THE O
OF ANATOLE FRANCE

Recorded by Paul Gsell
Translated from the French
by Ernest Boyd

New York
ALFRED ˒A˒ KNOPF
1922

Anatole France

From a photograph by Eduard J. Steichen

Contents

To the Reader

To The Reader

The familiar discourses of the Abbé Jérôme
Coignard have been preserved for us by his ingenu-
ous disciple Jacques Tournebroche. My excellent
Master, Anatole France, has a certain spiritual re-
lationship with the Abbé Jérôme Coignard. His
discourse is no less elegant. It would be a pity,
indeed, if his learned and weighty sayings were lost
for ever. Like another Tournebroche, it was my
good fortune to treasure them at those erstwhile
gatherings in the Villa Saïd, which were the most
dazzling feasts of reason, during the years before
the war. Thither came men of letters, artists,
statesmen, Spanish anarchists and Russian nihilists.
With his keen delight in knowing the strangest
specimens of humanity, the master of the house received them all with affectionate courtesy. The
attraction of his own personality saved him the
necessity of going in search of game. The models
which he wanted to draw came to his house and
posed for him without any compulsion. He did
them the signal favour of trying on them some of
the most ingenious apophthegms which he after-

wards put down in writing. It was this prepara-
tory work of a great artist in his studio which it
was my privilege to follow for many years.

When Anatole France is mentioned it is usual
to say: "He is a magician, but what a dreadful
sceptic!" As one who listened to him assiduously,
I can correct this too prevalent misunderstanding.

If by a sceptic is meant a philosopher who doubts
what he does not know to be true, and what he has
no reason whatever to believe, who mocks at fatal
prejudices, makes fun of swollen reputations, and
lashes stupid and cruel ambitions, then, assuredly,
Anatole France is the prince of sceptics. But it is
just the contrary of the truth to say that he is indifferent to all things. I had no difficulty in discovering very solid convictions in his slightest re-
torts.

He is perhaps the last craftsman of letters who
has retained the fine superstition of a fluid and
diaphanous style, the noble prejudice in favour of
words full of savour, and of harmonious phrases.
He loves gentle France so piously that he has made
of that tender word a pseudonym in order to be
at one with his country. Like the most generous
minds of his native land, he professes the religion
of sincerity, the cult of tolerance and devotion to
pity. Experience has been far from indulgent to
his hopes. Yet, during the worst periods of de-

To the Reader

pression in his lifetime he has preserved his faith in the slow and certain progress of justice and goodness. When occasion arose, this nonchalant dreamer did not spare himself, nor hesitate to go into the market-place to defend the Ideal. Heaven knows what an effort it is for him to take off his crimson skull cap and his blanket-wool dressing gown, kick off his slippers and leave his fireside. Many a time, however, he has left his ivory tower with resolute step to bring words of good cheer to his rough comrades in the working-class districts.

Finally, he adores friendship above everything else. Thus, the man who symbolizes incredulity in the eyes of many of his contemporaries is, after his own fashion, the most devout believer. Such is the evidence of his own words in the pages which follow.

Here in their first form will be found not only maxims with which he embellished his writings, but also many excellent and hitherto unpublished stories. No doubt, these are but the crumbs and fragments of a royal feast, but the superior quality of great men is not always attested in their most laboured works. Rather may it be recognized in what springs spontaneously and without effort from their brain. The best of their genius often lies in what they never think of writing down, but reveal in instinctive outbursts, in thoughts long matured,

The Opinions of Anatole France

which come out involuntarily, without their noticing it.

As is well known, M. France is the most perfect talker. His novels, after all, are little more than philosophical dialogues held together by a tenuous thread. Probably his most attractive book is the delightful *Jardin d'Epicure,* where he scatters his idle fancies like the petals of a flower. The present work represents an adjacent field of fancy. It will certainly give less pleasure, because the hand of the wizard himself does not guide the pen. I have endeavoured, however, to preserve even the form of his speech. Already for some time before the war bitter troubles had inclined Anatole France towards isolation. The awful cyclone drove him from Versailles, where he had sought repose amidst the nostalgic splendours of the past. He transferred his household goods to La Béchellerie, a small property which he acquired near Tours, and where he lived in meditation during the years of horror.

His spirit has been saddened by so many catastrophes. The interminable butchery was a cruel trial for a heart overflowing with human compassion. There is little likelihood that my excellent Master will ever resume those meetings at which his mocking humour sparkled, and so, I no longer postpone the task of catching something of its elusive memory.

The Hermitage of the Sage

The Hermitage of the Sage

Prancing in the silvery morning sunlight fashionable ladies on horseback and skilled horsemen come down from the Arc de Triomphe towards the Porte Dauphine along the Avenue du Bois de Boulogne. From one side of that proud thoroughfare there runs a blind alley, quiet and planted with sycamores, which a diligent gardener has pruned and trimmed in the French fashion. This is the Villa Saïd. The dwelling-houses along the side are of modest height, and have a rural air, although they are within the city boundaries of Paris. They are attractive and well cared for behind their iron railings, and they shelter gentle folk, people of private means, artists, authors and philosophers. Anatole France lives at number five.

For a long time during the war this house was silent, abandoned by its master. It seemed widowed and melancholy. The door, the windows on the ground floor, were hideously barricaded with bricks and plaster. It was the picture of desolation. Since then this gloomy façade has opened its windows again, as though they were eyelids, and smiles

The Opinions of Anatole France

once more. Sometimes Anatole France returns to his hermitage, when he is not staying at Saint-Cyr-lès-Tours on the banks of the Loire, or with friends beneath the shady trees of Saint-Cloud. But I wish to describe this little house at the Villa Saïd, the Hermitage of the Sage, as it was in the happy times when crowds of visitors haunted it.

The green painted door was a museum in itself. The handle of the bell was in bronze, a little Florentine head, whose grace seemed to give a friendly reception to the hand that caressed it. The letter box was studded with old medals. One day the master himself showed me over the house.

The old servant, Joséphine, had admitted me. She was a worthy servitor for M. Bergeret. She always wore a rather mistrustful expression. She would open the door a couple of inches, look at the newcomer suspiciously, keep him prudently outside during this minute inspection, and allow him to enter only when she knew who it was.

Every day little pieces of pasteboard were handed to her on which she would decipher the names of dukes, marquises, generals, academicians and statesmen. Human greatness was only too familiar to Joséphine. She had seen through the vanity of it all.

"Is the Master at home?" people would ask.

The Hermitage of the Sage

"The Master! The Master!" she would repeat grumbling: "Why do you call him Master? He is master only of his soup, and even of that only so long as he has it in his mouth."

She would mumble these savoury phrases between her gold-filled teeth. It was not unpleasant to hear the servant of a philosopher uttering opinions so full of sap.

The hall was overflowing with treasures. Persian china with blue, green and red carnations; pottery from Rhodes with bronzed lights; ancient statuettes standing on small tables and consoles. A fat monk was hastily telling his beads near a German Virgin with protruding forehead and crinkly hair. A mincing Italian Lucretia was eternally piercing her breast.

Through the gold-spangled stained-glass windows an iridescent light fell upon the staircase. From the very threshold one could recognize the taste of a most learned and discriminating collector. This hall, so sumptuously decorated, recalled an anecdote I had heard.

A young girl student from Russia had no other thought, on arriving in Paris, than to see Anatole France. From the writer's fame and his books she worshipped this friend of the humble and suffering, and, furnished with a warm recommendation, she rushed off to the Villa Saïd.

The Opinions of Anatole France

She hands her letter to Joséphine who goes up one floor to tell her master. He consents to receive the visitor.

"Come up!" shouts the servant peremptorily across the banisters.

But there is no reply.

Joséphine comes down again, rather impatient. The hall is empty. She looks in the dining-room, the drawing-room. Nobody there.

Well! What is wrong, Joséphine? asks the master who is waiting.

"Well, Sir, I don't know where in the world the young lady has disappeared."

What?

"She has decamped."

What on earth do you mean?

"I can't make it out, Sir. I have looked every-where. I can't find her. She has gone!"

Well, upon my word! She must be mad!

Later on the riddle was explained. As soon as she entered, the Russian girl was dumbfounded by a refinement of luxury which exceeded the opulence of the most magnificent Crœsus. It was not thus that she had pictured the retreat of an apostle. This simple soul, this candid child of Scythia, could not conceive that a passion for the Beautiful was compatible with a tender heart. She had been seized by a kind of anguish. Suddenly, she had turned about, and gone out. She had quietly closed the door behind her and had fled, even more quickly than she had come. She was never seen again.

I took good care not to imitate that Russian student, and as soon as ever Joséphine shouted to me, I hastened upstairs to the philosopher's study.

Anatole France was about to submit his head to the attentions of the barber, and with a courtesy which I deeply appreciated, he apologized for continuing his toilet in my presence.

Figaro, who came forward with his razor opened and the shaving-soap, spilt some of the lather on the table and scattered a few pages of manuscript. France stared at him with an expression of comic irritation.

You always come in here like a scythed chariot. You are a terrible man.

Doubtless accustomed to these lyrical outbursts, the terrible man did not utter a sound, but prepared to begin operations. It was not an easy task, for M. Bergeret kept moving and talking all the time while his beard was being trimmed. In one of his tales Grimm tells of a barber who was so skilful that he could shave a hare in full flight. That was child's play beside the miracle of which I was a witness.

The bedroom was charming. Above the Renaissance bed an Italian canopy was supported by twisted brown columns, and its green silk was brightened with flowers of tender hue. Amongst the things which he liked best, France pointed to a piece of antique sculpture on the mantelpiece. It was a woman's head, thrown back a little, with half-closed eyes filled with amorous languor.

I discovered it, he said, *on the seashore near Naples, in a fishermen's hut which was almost entirely built of broken fragments of masterpieces. It was some distance from my hotel, so I added another lira to the price agreed upon, to have this piece of marble, which is very heavy, carried for me. At first I did not notice who was going to do it, but suddenly I remarked that it was a poor woman, in an advanced stage of pregnancy. I hastened to relieve her of this burden and to give it to a young lad whom I presented in advance with another small silver coin. Now, observe how one's best intentions are misunderstood. The good fisherwoman was so annoyed at being paid for a service of which I relieved her that she interpreted my compassion as an insult. She did not return the lira, which I certainly would not have taken back, but she followed me all along the road hurling vulgar insults at me. Thus, I learnt that honesty is deeply rooted in the heart of man . . . and even of woman.*

The Hermitage of the Sage

That is not the only memory which that voluptuous head recalls.

I left Naples by sea. As you know, the Italians make sure that travellers do not carry off works of art in their trunks. A wise ordinance, the Pacca law, prohibits the spoliation of the artistic marvels of which the peninsula is so proud. I wanted that head and I had made up my mind not to declare it. I had carefully packed it in a little white wooden box. When the customs inspector asked what was in that package:

"Niente! Niente!" said I, very innocently.

He accepted this evasive reply, and was going to put the little box amongst the things which had already been examined. But alas! the bottom fell out, and when the box was lifted, the head suddenly appeared, with its expression of ecstatic love, and seemed to defy the world. I was covered with shame. The inspector examined the piece of marble like an expert, struck an attitude to contemplate it, and then turned to me with an ineffable smile:

"Niente! Niente!" he said mockingly.

The cruel monster was torturing me. But with superior condescension he said:

"Take it. We have too many beautiful things in Italy."

The Opinions of Anatole France

You would have thought that this excise man had carved with his own hands all the Venuses of antiquity, and that he could create others by the dozen.

When his beard was finished France stood up and put on his scarlet cap exactly like those of the Quattrocento Florentines, in the frescoes with which Ghirlandajo has embellished the church of Santa-Maria Novella.

We entered his study.

On the table an adorable winged spirit of Tanagra rose upon its toes to take flight.

I think it is genuine, said my host, *and, what is still better, it is delightful.*

With a reverent hand he took the little Cupid and, raising it to his eyes, almost to his lips, he caressed it tenderly. A dialogue without words between a very modern thinker and the naïve modeller who, in the distant past, had impregnated this clay with all the melancholy grace of his time.

M. Bergeret has eclectic tastes and his purchases prove their variety.

The fact is, his preferences varied from year to year, and his domestic surroundings were modified according to the books he was writing. Each period of his life has left rich alluvial deposits. *Thaïs* is represented by the relics of Hellas, the heads, and torsos, the statuettes and the slender

The Hermitage of the Sage

pedestals of amber-coloured marble; the *Lys Rouge* by Italian faïence; *Jeanne d' Arc* by the fifteenth century tapestries; the novel, *Les Dieux ont soif,* by furniture and engravings dating from Louis XVI and the Revolution. The style which finally dominated was that of the end of the Eighteenth Century, because it harmonized with the last avatar of that infinitely capricious sensitiveness. This house reflects a soul in its decorations. It is a setting like the elegant case in which a wonderful jewel is enchased.

I am not wealthy, France explains, *and yet my collection is very creditable. Collectors are like lovers, passion makes up for want of money. Beautiful women are often more deeply touched by the fervent and insistent prayers of poor swains than by the dazzling liberality of financiers rolling in wealth.*

In the boxes of the second-hand book dealers, in the half-closed portfolios at the back of dark shops, the unique items, which the millionaires miss, sometimes cast inviting glances at those who browse with ill-furnished purses, but who seek, pursue, run down and implore them with frantic covetousness.

However, for the conquest of women and masterpieces it is better to be both rich and passionate.

.　　.　　.　　.　　.　　.　　.　　.

[23]

The Opinions of Anatole France

M. Bergeret showed us his old books.

I love them tenderly, because they bring forget-fulness of the present and a little inoffensive madness to those who consult them. This little grain of madness affects even those who handle them without reading them. For instance, I don't know a gayer spirit than the excellent Sims, the bookseller in the Rue de Seine, who sold me most of these folios. He has two equally praiseworthy loves: the best ancient authors and the generous wines of France. When he confides in me that he has just made an extraordinary discovery, I never know if he means a dusty bottle or exceedingly rare incunabula. He often goes about strangely dressed, but that comes from reasoned principles. He holds that the order in which we put on our clothes is a pure convention. For his part, on getting up in the morning he picks up his things haphazardly from the chair. He may happen to put on his coat first, then his shirt, then his waistcoat, and finally his flannel undervest on top of everything.

"What does it matter," he says, "provided the amount of clothes is the same? Am I not just as warm?"

Although this a specious theory, I do not attempt to refute it, for it would be too much trouble to convince him. The other day I found him all stuffed up with a cold, sneezing, coughing, wiping his nose, puffing and snorting; his nose and eyes running like fountains.

"Well, my good Sims, where did you catch that dreadful cold?"

"I do not know. I have not been careless in any way, not in the least."

Thereupon he told me that he had bought a big lot of books the previous evening. But there was no room in his shop, so he had to take them up to his bedroom, which was already very full. He had even been obliged to pile up a great many on the very foot of his bed. The drawback of this stratagem he discovered when he was going to sleep. Fortunately, the head of his bed was against the window, and the window looked out upon the roof. He could think of nothing better than to open the window and pull up his mattress a little onto the slates. After that, with his body in the room and his head outside, the good man fell into a childlike slumber.

Alas, what should happen but, in the middle of the night, a furious storm broke out, and all the cataracts of heaven descended upon his head.

"Oh, I see," said I. "So that is how you caught cold."

"Do you really think so?" . . . he inquired.

The Opinions of Anatole France

What I like about Sims is that he accepts the most convincing arguments only with extreme caution.

France reverently took from a shelf a very beautiful book, covered with parchment, golden-brown, like old ivory, and decorated with the figures of fabulous animals.

This Vasari is my pride, he said.

He turned the pages and came to the portrait of Paolo Uccello.

This is the painter whose wife gently reproached him with working too slowly.

"I must have time," the artist said, "to establish the perspective of my pictures."

"Yes, Paolo," the poor woman protested, "but you are drawing for us the perspective of destitution and the grave."

She was right, and he was not wrong. The eternal conflict between the scruples of the artist and harsh reality.

Thus M. Bergeret plunged into the peaceful fairyland of past centuries far from contemporary cares, daily disappointments, and the threats which were rising on the horizon. By means of pictures, sculptures and books he was in communication with the dead. With these written signs, these painted and carved forms, he endeavoured to penetrate to the souls of other times. Eager for knowledge,

The Hermitage of the Sage

he annexed innumerable days that were gone to the hours he was living. According to his custom, it was in his dressing gown and slippers that he accomplished an immense circuit through time, bringing back fruitful teaching for us.

Joséphine came in to announce two delegates from a Socialist committee.

·One was a big red-faced man, conventionally dressed, but wearing a soft shirt and no tie, for his powerful neck could stand no other restraint. He was a blacksmith. He apologized for not offering his right hand, which was bandaged, because it had been injured in some workshop job. His companion, small and sickly, with burning eyes and tousled hair, was a school teacher. The one in his brutal strength, and the other in his feverish weakness, personified the people, condemned to laborious drudgery of mind and body. They congratulated France on having spoken at a recent meeting.

His speech had raised storms of applause, but it had been continually punctuated by shouts of "Long live anarchy!" This compromising cry had been shouted in chorus by a group of police spies obviously recognizable by their huge moustaches, their degraded faces and their hobnailed boots. The two delegates warmly condemned the tactics of the *agents provocateurs*.

[27]

The Opinions of Anatole France

They asked the author to take the chair at another meeting.

He looked at his slippers, patted his Vasari, gave a furtive and benevolent glance at the little Tanagra Cupid. Then his dark eyes rested for a moment on the bandaged wrist of the blacksmith and the hollow cheeks of the schoolmaster.

I will go, he said.

Candidates for the Academy

Candidates for the Academy

As every election to the Academy approaches the candidates pay their prescribed visit to M. Bergeret. They know that he has not gone to that corner of the quays this many a year, and that he never votes. Nevertheless out of deference to his fame they solicit his vote. It is a touching custom which none seeks to evade, not even the reverend clergy. Yet, they would have valid reasons for not committing themselves with this pontiff of incredulity. But perhaps his conversation offers them the attraction of forbidden fruit? Perhaps they hope in a few eloquent words to cast into his soul the seeds of a startling conversion? It was thus that the severe Paphnuce once upon a time undertook to bring the frolicsome Thaïs to God.

When Cardinal Cabrières, who was still only a Monsignor, but was soon to become His Eminence, craved a chair in the Academy, he called like the others at the hermitage of the Villa Saïd.

Old Joséphine, with her teeth of gold, ushered him in with every mark of respect.

"Sir," said the bishop brusquely, "I will admit

to you frankly that I have not read your novels."

"*Monsignor*," replied France, with sacerdotal unction, "*I must confess to you in all frankness that I have not read your decrees.*"

The ice having been broken in this way, the conversation became cordial. The prelate paternally reminded France that some great writers had sung the praise of the Almighty. He cited Chateaubriand.

France retorted that, in effect, the harmonious viscount had beautifully celebrated the decorative side of Catholicism, but above all he had dusted the furniture and polished the ecclesiastical plate, like a beadle or a chair attendant, and that, on the other hand, he had rather neglected dogma.

He loved the majesty of the cathedrals and the splendor of the ritual pomps. But I, too, love them, Monsignor.

With a devout gesture he pointed to the golden stoles, the coruscating chasubles, the bright silver incense boxes, which were glittering in their glass cases.

Chateaubriand venerated the sacred authors. I also feast upon them, Monsignor.

On the shelves of the library, in the place of honour, he showed him the Eagle of Meaux and the Swan of Cambrai dwelling happily together.

He looked as if butter would not melt in his

mouth. Monsignor de Cabrières withdrew, convinced that, in some respects, the most fervent of believers would gain by taking lessons from Anatole France.

The following Wednesday—for it was on Wednesday that M. Bergeret received his intimate friends—they spoke of Monsignor Duchesne who was the rival candidate of Monsignor de Cabrières for the Academy. The rivalry of the two prelates amused the onlookers. Bets were taken. Two to one was laid on Monsignor Duchesne. The sympathies of the academic Left wing for the one and of the Right for the other were weighed in the balance. Some one told the story of the scurvy trick played by the author of *Les Origines de la France chrétienne* on Monsignor de Cabrières, who was a splendid orator, but had written practically nothing.

Monsignor Duchesne had gone into several bookshops near the Mazarin Palace, and had said in the most innocent tones:

"Give me the complete works of Monsignor de Cabrières."

The shop assistants were amazed.

"The complete works of Monsignor de Cabrières? We haven't them in stock."

"Oh, yes, you must have. Have a look!"

They searched and then:

"We cannot find them, Monsignor."

The Opinions of Anatole France

"Come now, Monsignor de Cabrières is a candidate for the Academy. He must have surely written something, and I want particularly to read his books. Look again, please."

Great commotion. The owners and their assistants searched everywhere, moving piles of books and climbing ladders. But still there was nothing.

"We are very sorry, Monsignor!"

"So am I! So am I!"

As he went out he raised his hands to heaven.

"Where, oh, where shall I find the complete works of Monsignor de Cabrières?"

This prank, duly reported by the booksellers, delighted the honourable members of the Academy. That morning some one had related the story, while it was still new, to M. Bergeret, who smacked his lips over it, and said:

Monsignor Duchesne has always had a fine sense of humour. Before he received the amethyst ring, he used to live on the third floor, on the Quai Voltaire. One of his archaeological colleagues called on him, and in a transport of joy announced that he had discovered a new saint while deciphering some old cartularies.

"Pshaw!" cried the Abbé bluntly, "your saint is legendary; like so many others, my dear Sir, he has never existed." And he learnedly set forth the

Candidates for the Academy

reasons for this opinion. They simply exasperated his visitor.

"Sir," he said furiously, "your rudeness betrays your Breton origins. You remind me of your ancestors, savage Armorican pirates, who ransacked the shores of the sea. No more of this! All I ask of you is to tell me where is the nearest landing place of the river steamboats."

"Sir," the Abbé answered haughtily, "I should be insulting the dignity of my ancestors were I to trouble about fresh water craft."

You will agree that there was a great deal of subtlety in this retort of an offended archaeologist.

One of us recalled the witticisms attributed to Monsignor Duchesne, the joke, for instance, about the naïve politics of Pope Pius X.

"He is a Venetian gondolier in the barque of Saint Peter. He guides it *à la gaffe*."[1] And the other one.

"Have you read the latest Bull: *Digitus in oculo?*"

It is not at all certain, Anatole France resumed, *that those jokes are his. But, to him that hath shall be given. No doubt Monsignor Duchesne is too witty for a priest, and such flights may perhaps*

[1] *An untranslatable pun on the word "Gaffe," which means "blunder" as well as the pole with which a gondolier steers his craft.*

*do him wrong. But he has more serious matters
to worry about.*

*One day, when he was walking in Rome with the
famous archaeologist Rossi they came to a halt
in front of a beautiful marble tablet, recently
affixed, and on which was engraved in Latin: "On
this spot the apostles Saint Peter and Saint Paul
met." The historical incredibility of the event
made them shake their heads. Above this sentence
they read in Italian: "It is strictly forbidden to de-
posit rubbish against this wall."*

"A wise order," said Rossi.

*". . . but not very strictly obeyed!" added the
Abbé, pointing with his walking stick to the hagio-
graphical inscription." And the two interlocutors
resumed their walk.*

Anatole France continued.

*The physical resemblance between Monsignor
Duchesne and Voltaire is striking. I conclude . . .
that Voltaire was a holy man.*

But, some one asked, how does Monsignor
Duchesne reconcile his faith and his erudition?

FRANCE.—*He does not reconcile them. Why
should he reconcile them? He is at the same time
very learned and very pious. His Catholicism and
his archaeology dwell together in his soul as mutual
strangers. They are separated by a water-tight
compartment. And do not imagine that his case is*

Candidates for the Academy

exceptional. Beneath the skull of every one of us a crowd of contradictory ideas are sheltered. We are attached to them all equally and they get on very well because we never allow them to meet.

. . . .

At this moment M. Edmond Haraucourt entered, the truculent poet of *La Légende des sexes,* and keeper of the Cluny Museum.

He began with a few compliments.

"My dear Master," he said, "I am delighted to see you looking so young."

FRANCE.—*Ha ha! I am growing old, all the same.*

"Oh Master," protested a very nice young man who had not previously opened his mouth, "if you are growing old there is not the slightest sign of it in your recent books."

FRANCE. (maliciously)—*Good heavens! In my books! That would be the last straw! . . . There are, alas! other signs by which I recognize my enemy, Old Age. You will know them later, very much later, young man, you who rise triumphantly every morning.* (Turning to M. Haraucourt.) *Well, my dear keeper, how is your Museum?*

HARAUCOURT.—"I keep weeding it out, removing the parasites. . . ."

FRANCE.—*What?*

HARAUCOURT.—"It is full of fakes."

[37]

The Opinions of Anatole France

FRANCE.—*Yes, indeed. I suspected as much.*

HARAUCOURT.—"Thanks to strict supervision, I am separating the wheat from the chaff. Everything that looks dubious I remove from the Museum to the keeper's house."

FRANCE.—*An excellent idea.*

HARAUCOURT.—"The furniture which I have got together in this way for my personal use is plentiful and hideous. My apartment has become the sanctuary of fakes, the Pantheon of cheap imitations. But I shall have to modify my critical rigour, for my drawing-room, dining-room, bedroom and even my W. C. are packed with Boulle cabinets, Louis XIII clocks, and Henry II buffets all genuine XIXth century." [2]

We were all laughing.

M. Haraucourt continued:

"Lately I had the most tremendous and unwelcome surprise. You know our famous fourteenth century coffer, so greatly praised in the handbooks on art?"

FRANCE.—*I certainly do.*

HARAUCOURT.—"It is a fake!"

FRANCE.—*Well, I never!*

[2] *This heterogeneous furniture has since been distributed once more through the Museum for M. Haraucourt does not live there any longer.*

Candidates for the Academy

HARAUCOURT.—"This is the way I discovered it. I wanted to celebrate this coffer in verse, for it inspired me. On the wooden panels some designs are carved which I thought I recognized as the *Joyes du Mariage*. A married couple are squabbling and abusing one another. The good wives are decorating their husbands' foreheads with luxurious branches. I had tuned my lute and was strumming a prelude, when I noticed on two sides heroic scenes which had nothing in common with the others. There were knights, with lances in their hands, setting out for war. I know, of course, that military men can gallantly intervene in civilian households, but there were really too many of these paladins. I began to smell a rat. I discovered that my coffer is an artificial tinkering together of scraps and odds and ends. Only a third of the cover goes back to the fourteenth century. You can imagine how I dropped my lute. But for heaven's sake gentlemen, be discreet! This coffer is our glory. It is so famous that I could not bring myself to deprive the public of it."

France laughed until the tears rolled down his cheeks.

"You would never guess," Haraucourt resumed, "that I am paying you my visit as a candidate for the Academy."

The Opinions of Anatole France

FRANCE.—*Do you not know that I never put my foot inside the Mazarin Palace?* [3]

HARAUCOURT.—"Come, my dear Master, could you not. . . ."

FRANCE.—*Listen, my friend. Even the ushers would not recognize me. By the way, here is a good idea. . . . Let me introduce my Russian friend Semenoff. . . .*

SEMENOFF.—(A giant with a great black beard, bows to M. Haraucourt.)

"Monsieur. . . ."

HARAUCOURT (bowing)—."Monsieur. . . ."

FRANCE.—*My friend Semenoff could go in my place to the Academy, and say that he is Anatole France. . . . No; seriously, it would not look well if I were to go there only for the purpose of voting.*

HARACOURT.—"At all events, thanks for your platonic vote!"

FRANCE.—*My poor friend!—You must certainly have more effective supporters. Come, who are they? Let us run over the names of the Academicians. The worst of it is one hardly knows them.*

HARAUCOURT.—"I give you my word! Every

---

[3] *During the war, as a mark of respect to the sacred union, M. Anatole France appeared at the Academy. But he soon forgot to find his way back.*

[40]

Candidates for the Academy

time there is a vacancy half-a-dozen poor devils can
be counted in Paris, who learn off the complete list
of the Immortals, and who go from apartment to
apartment, ringing the bell."

FRANCE.—*In order to console you, shall I re-
call the delightful pages in the "Journal d'un
Poètè," in which Vigny has recorded his visit to
Royer-Collard?*

HARAUCOURT.—"I know them by heart. What
delicious fooling! Old Royer-Collard wrapped
up in his dressing gown like Geronte, with a
black wig on his head, half opens the door to
Vigny and says: 'I cannot be seen, Sir, I have just
taken a dose of medicine.' And he adds: 'Between ourselves, you have not the slightest chance
—Besides, I know nothing of your works, for I
have read nothing now for thirty years. . . . At
my age, Sir, one no longer reads. One re-reads.'"

FRANCE.—*Well, my dear friend, you see to
what humiliation the candidature of the noble
Vigny exposed his pride . . . May his example help
you patiently to bear your own tribulations.*

On Becoming An Academician

On Becoming An Academician

"It is certain," Haraucourt resumed, "that nothing has changed since Vigny's time. He complained that Royer-Collard had not read his works, and in the course of my visits I perceive that very few of the Immortals are acquainted with my literary impedimenta. It is most depressing!"

FRANCE.—*What did you expect? Never, never in the world, have the Academicians opened the works of the candidates. Look at Leconte de Lisle, the blasphemer who wrote "Poèmes Barbares"; he was elected as a Christian poet, I assure you. I know what I am talking about. I followed his election minute by minute. I was secretary of the Senate Library when he was Chief Librarian.*

It was thanks to the Duc de Broglie that he was elected. The Duc de Broglie knew that Leconte de Lisle was a poet. How did he find that out? That is what I am still wondering.

"I have been told about a poet," he confided to his colleagues.

The Opinions of Anatole France

Here France's voice became piping and tremulous in imitation of the Duc de Broglie.

"This poet is certainly a spiritualist, for all poets are. Spiritualism and Christianity, are one and the same. This chap Leconte de Lisle is, therefore, a Christian, a good Christian, an excellent Christian. I am voting for him. You do likewise."

You must understand that the Duc de Broglie carried Christianity to the point of crime. He had an amorous temperament. One day his doctor advised him to take a mistress in order to spare his wife, whose health was very precarious.

The Duc reflected for a while and then said suddenly.

"Well, after all, my dear doctor, I had much rather imperil my wife than my immortal soul."

Furthermore, the election of Leconte de Lisle was facilitated by a fortunate error. The majority of the immortals who voted in his favour, I am told, attributed to him Sully Prudhomme's "Le Vase brisé".

M. Haraucourt's face expressed the utmost bewilderment.

FRANCE.—*But most of the time, as you know, my dear friend, as well as I do, the elections are purely political.*

On Becoming An Academician

HARAUCOURT.—Yet, my dear Master, your own was not!

FRANCE.—*On the contrary, it was so more than any other. But the story is worth telling in detail.*

Ludovic Halévy, who loved me like a brother, kept constantly saying: "Why sulk at the Academy? It is the thing to join. It looks well on the covers of one's books. Present yourself. Do it for my sake. I am ashamed to be an Immortal when you are not." Well, the end of it was that I drew up my letter of application, and went to read it to him.

"Tut, tut!" said he, "your letter is not in due form. Give it to me and I will arrange it properly." And he deliberately inserted three or four fearful mistakes in French, which stood out like poppies in a corn field.

"There," he said, "is the style required. But that is not everything. We must find out who will vote for you."

He drew up a list and proceeded to tick off a great number of names.

"Hm! Hm!" he muttered, "it will not be easy. These damned aristocrats will make wry faces when they have to swallow you."

I began making my calls. Halévy directed operations. Every morning I received a note: "Go

The Opinions of Anatole France

'to So and So! Call again on So and So!" All
the time he was consumed with anxiety. Finally,
one day when I saw him he was radiant.

"That's all right!" said he, rubbing his hands,
"we've got them!"

"Got whom?"

"The aristocrats! Listen. There are two seats
vacant. The extreme Left of the Academy is
putting you forward for one. The aristocrats have
a candidate for the other, a worthy nobleman of
ancient lineage, but an absolute illiterate. They
will not find it easy to push him through.

"We said to them: Do you want the extreme
Left to vote for your nobleman? Then, vote
for the anarchist, Anatole France. One good turn
deserves another. It's a bargain! They agreed.
I am delighted. Now, call on the nobility. They
have been warned. But for heaven's sake, don't
talk politics or religion! Say: What bright sun-
shine! or: It is windy! It is raining! It is driz-
gling! Ask the lady of the house how her little dog
is and her pet monkeys. The noblemen have been
similarly instructed."

Everything turned out as he had foreseen. The
anarchist and the nobleman were elected on the
same day and by the same votes. It was quite shame-
less.

· · · · · · ·

[48]

On Becoming An Academician

HARAUCOURT.—It does not matter. The Academy honoured itself by electing you.

FRANCE (shaking hands with him)—*Thanks my dear friend. But that is not all. There is a sequel.*

Amongst the votes promised to me, only one was missing, Henri de Bornier's. As this little act of treason was divulged, he tried to apologize to me.

"Dear Monsieur France," he began, "I did not vote for you."

"I beg your pardon, Monsieur de Bornier, you did vote for me."

"No, I did not," he replied, somewhat taken aback.

"But, you did. You are a gentleman, are you not, Monsieur de Bornier?"

"Certainly, but. . . ."

"Have you not sung the praise of honour?"

"No doubt, but. . . ."

"It is, therefore, impossible for you to have broken your word. You did vote for me, Monsieur de Bornier, you did."

"He went off like a dog with its tail between its legs. But my vengeance was not complete. . .I was only waiting for an opportunity to satisfy my thirst for revenge. The opportunity came when we were in session on the dictionary. . . .

My dear Haraucourt, you will certainly take

[49]

The Opinions of Anatole France

part in the dictionary sessions. For you will be elected. One always gets what one ardently desires.

HARAUCOURT.—You never can tell!

FRANCE.—*You need have no doubts on that score! And I hope you will be pleasantly diverted by these famous sessions.*

We never got any further than the letter A, for they do a very short day's work at the Academy. The entry after Anneau (Ring) was being made, and the Duc de Broglie was presiding. By a majority of votes the following definition was adopted:

Ring: a piece of metal circular in shape.

"Smoke ring," I whispered insidiously.

These words caused some disturbance, but a grammarian replied with great assurance:

"All right. We will put: by catachresis: smoke ring."

Catachresis seemed to be a sublime idea.

As an example, the Ring of Saturn was quoted.

"The astronomers have discovered several of them," I observed. "So you will have to say the Rings of Saturn."

"No," they said, "it is customary to say the Ring of Saturn. We are here only to ratify usage. So much the worse for your astronomers!"

This annoyed me, and it was then that I conceived an infernal idea.

[50]

On Becoming An Academician

The chair next to mine just happened to be dear old Bornier's. He was snoring loudly. I nudged him with my elbow:

"They are forgetting Hans Carvel's ring."

"What!" he cried, rubbing his eyes.

At this point France opened a parenthesis.

I suppose you all know that ribald story. You have read it in the third book of Pantagruel. The good man, Hans Carvel, married late in life to a frisky wench, was tortured by jealousy. One night when he was sleeping beside his wife, the devil came in a dream and offered him a lovely ring: "Put this ring on your finger. As long as it is there, your spouse will be faithful."

In his joy the good man wakes up, and hears his wife saying: "Stop! Stop! That will do!"

Accustomed to unsheath Durandal, to sound the horn of battle, to bestride Pegasus, and to prance in the clouds, Henri de Bornier had never read Rabelais.

I repeated to him:

"They are forgetting Hans Carvel's ring. You had better tell them."

Immediately the worthy old gentleman cried out in his innocence:

"Gentlemen, you are forgetting Hans Carvel's ring."

There were a few laughs.

The Opinions of Anatole France

The Duc de Broglie, who knew his Rabelais perfectly, but who was of a serious disposition, checked this unseemly laughter at once.

"Let us continue, gentlemen," he said sharply.

A moment later I leaned over to Bornier:

"They did not hear you," said I.

"Gentlemen, gentlemen," he cried, very much agitated, "you are forgetting Hans Carvel's ring."

This time there was a storm of laughter.

"What on earth is the matter with them?" Bornier asked me.

"I don't know," I replied hypocritically.

The Duc de Broglie was furious and declared the session at an end.

As we went out, he came beside me:

"An extraordinary man, Bornier is," he said to me. "A fine name of good ancestry, an old Périgord family, but he is too fond of the bottle. And, by Jove, when he has had a glass too many, he tells dirty stories that would bring a blush to the face of a brass monkey."

That, my dear Haraucourt, is the veracious story of my election to the French Academy, and of the curious episode connected therewith.

France continued:

The Immortals read nothing. They crown their new colleagues without having ever opened their

On Becoming An Academician

works. They distribute literary prizes on the same principle, for they find it works. Sometimes, however, it leads them into some strange blunders.

Do you know, my dear Haraucourt, the story of a poetry prize awarded to Louise Colet?

"No," he replied.

He would have said no, even if he had known it, for he is a man of courtesy.

FRANCE.—*Under the Second Empire Louise Colet was a majestic female, very beautiful, rather a virago, with a man's voice, and eyes which she knew how to use. She was married to a very ugly little dwarf, who played the violin at the Conservatory. The great philosopher, Victor Cousin, when he saw her, discovered in her the Good, the True and the Beautiful. He reduced the little violinist to the same plight as Sganarelle. It was the correct thing to do.*

Louise Colet used to twang the lyre. She asked her metaphysician to have some poetry prizes awarded her by the French Academy. How could Cousin refuse such a modest recompense for divine hours? So, every year that God granted, Louise Colet used to get her prize. It was as regular as clockwork.

On one occasion the good lady began rather late to manufacture her piece for the competition. The night before the last day for receiving entries she had not hatched a single line. She was greatly embarrassed.

That night there were some artists and writers at her dinner table. It chanced that Flaubert and Bouilhet had come. They were fond of her, because she was an amiable creature and made everybody feel comfortable. After dinner she shoved them into a corner of the drawing-room.

"My dears," said she, "you must save my life." And she revealed her predicament.

"Now you must be very nice. Follow me into my study. . . . This way. . . . Plant yourselves in those two excellent armchairs, and before midnight run me off two hundred lines on Immortality. That is the prescribed subject. Here are some paper and ink. . . . Oh, I was nearly forgetting! You will find tobacco and brandy in this cupboard." As a matter of fact, it was her custom to smoke and drink like a trooper.

Then she rejoined her other guests.

The two friends smoked and drank and chatted.

"By the way," cried Bouilhet towards eleven o'clock, "what about Immortality?"

"Oh, damn!" replied Flaubert.

And they returned to the brandy.

At a quarter to twelve Bouilhet begged Flaubert to begin to think about Immortality. Flaubert was still reluctant, but suddenly, seizing a copy of La-

On Becoming An Academician

martine on a shelf, he opened it at random. "Write this!" he ordered imperiously. And without stopping he dictated two hundred lines from "Les Harmonies."

When it was finished:

"Add the title: Immortality! . . . Excellent!

He was putting "Les Harmonies" back when Louise Colet appeared.

"Is it finished, my treasures?"

"Oh, yes. Certainly," said they, very lively.

She ran over the sheets of manuscript without recognizing Lamartine.

"You did not over-exert yourselves," said she, "but it will do, all the same. You are angels."

She gave them each a kiss. She presented her poem and got the prize, as usual, with many congratulations. The lines from Lamartine were printed over the name of Louise Colet. Nobody was any the wiser, for nobody read them.

Flaubert did not reveal the trick until very long afterwards.

Politics in the Academy

Politics in the Academy

"That is all very well, so far as the prizes of the Academy are concerned," M. Haraucourt remarked. "They are of little consequence, and I have no objection to the Immortals for not reading the elucubrations of the contestants. But when it comes to electing an Academician, it is a very different matter."

He was particularly perturbed by the intervention of politics. He returned to this subject and deplored it.

FRANCE.—*I am surprised that you should take this to heart. After all, what happens in the Academy is nothing new. Writers have almost always owed their success to politics.*

HARAUCOURT.—But you will have to admit that the charm and power of their style has had something to do with their fame.

FRANCE.—*It is just possible, my friend, that our ideas on the subject have remained rather those of the class-room. When bespectacled and hide-bound old pedants at school made us translate some Greek*

The Opinions of Anatole France

tragedy, ("Oedipus at Colonus," for example) they used to say:

"Note that charming second aorist.   Observe the conciseness of that genitive absolute.   The dignity of that optative is marvellous."

They used to din hundreds of similar remarks into our ears, until in the end we began to believe that it was the grammatical perfection of Sophocles which had aroused the enthusiasm of his contemporaries.   But there was one point which our gerund-grinders overlooked, namely, when Sophocles celebrated the name of Oedipus, the Theban hero whom the Athenians received with open arms when he was hooted by his own countrymen, the Greek dramatist's intention was to glorify Athens at the expense of Thebes, which had been its bitter enemy during the Peloponnesian war.

Bearing that knowledge in mind we can easily imagine what the first performance of "Oedipus at Colonus" was like, shortly after the death of the aged poet: the whole audience on their feet, interrupting every line with cheers, hissing the Thebans and stamping in frantic applause for this eulogy of their city.   And thus we discover the real reasons, the political reasons, for this enthusiasm.

When our venerable pedagogues used to comment upon "The Knights" of Aristophanes, they would carefully analyse the parabasis and point out the commutation, the anapests, the macron. And they taught us that this play was a perfect example of the style known as Old Comedy. But you will readily conceive that it had other attractions for the sailors of Piræus. What delighted them was to see Aristophanes grabbing Comrade Cleon by the seat of the trousers. The performance was punctuated with laughs and shouts and slaps. I suspect things were pretty rough. In a word, it was politics.

You will have to reconcile yourself to this, my dear Haraucourt. More often than not politics and literature merge into one. In Rome did not gentle Virgil do but propaganda for Augustus? And in our own country did not the author of the Cid become, in spite of himself, the adversary of Richelieu? Is not his censorious Emilie a flattering portrait of the Duchess de Chevreuse? Was Molière not the champion of the young King and the hard-working middle-class against the disturbed and dissatisfied nobility? People praise the irony of Voltaire, the sensitiveness of Diderot, the penetration of Montesquieu, the ruggedness of Rousseau. Their style is excellent. But, would they have received so much praise if their works had not been inexhaustible arsenals of political argument? What about the bewildering word juggling of Victor Hugo, the precious metal of his tinkling rhymes, his bold antitheses of black and white? Have they done as much for his glory as his invectives against Napoleon the Small? Nonsense, my dear fellow. You must admit that literature has very little to do with literary reputations.

HARAUCOURT.—Well, isn't that absurd?

FRANCE.—*No, indeed. It is not so absurd. Do you think that it shows any superiority on the part of scribblers that they should isolate themselves in some little corner and fumble for words, rehash epithets and polish phrases, without a thought for the world about them? I think it is rather an infirmity.*

As he spoke, we thought of the part he played in the famous Dreyfus Affair, still recent at the time, of his *Études d'Histoire contemporaine*, of the passionate harangues which he was constantly delivering at popular meetings.

It is right, he continued, *for an author to feel the pangs of common humanity, and sometimes to intervene in the quarrels of the market-place. Not that I think he should fawn on any party or have a finger in the electoral pie. I expect him to preserve the independence of his spirit, to dare always to tell the truth, and to denounce even the injustices committed by his own friends. I want him to soar unfettered. I wish his opinions to be hard upon selfish interests, but usually regarded as chimerical, and that they shall have no chance whatever of being*

Politics in the Academy

adopted for many a year. So far from spoiling his style courage will render it more proud and virile.

That, my dear Haraucourt, is why I do not consider the French Academy so culpable for taking part in politics.

"I beg your pardon, Master," said one of us, "it is wrong to take the wrong part."

France pushed his crimson cap onto the corner of his ear:

Will you tell me what exactly distinguishes the right from the wrong side in politics? Oh, yes! I see. . . . Our friends are on the right side; other people are on the wrong.

The Credo of a Sceptic

The Credo of a Sceptic

Anatole France was just on the point of publishing his *Jeanne d'Arc*. It had cost him twenty years of hard work. . . . Every page had been corrected, revised and rounded off like a piece of sculpture. That is the way the Master works. On looking at his manuscripts one is astounded to see how much labour has gone into that apparent facility and that easy gracefulness. It is a great lesson for novices.

He used to make incessant corrections, reversing sentences, making his transitions easier, cutting his sheets into pieces like a puzzle; and he would put at the beginning what was at the end, at the top what was at the bottom, then pasting it all together. Certain parts which had already been set by the printer were re-written and then re-set eight or ten times in proof. France would suppress a number of delightful touches. He sought and he achieved the utmost simplicity.

When the text was read in its first form his friends had said:

"It is really charming! It is exquisite! Do not touch it any more! You will spoil it all."

[67]

The Opinions of Anatole France

But as proof followed proof they had been forced to admit that there was continual progress in the direction of perfection. Yet, France could not bring himself to let this *Jeanne d'Arc* of his take flight on the wings of imagination. He had a suspicion that this work, conceived without any prejudice and respecting only the truth, would please but few readers. It was then that we found him in a melancholy mood.

He was chatting with Pierre Champion, the learned biographer of Charles d'Orleans and of François Villon. To this erudite young man he transferred the warm friendship which he used to show to his father, who died recently. The worthy publisher, Honoré Champion, of the Quai Malaquais, had indeed known the father of Anatole France, Thibault the bookseller, who had also kept a bookshop close by, on the Quai Voltaire, at the sign *Aux Armes de France*.

Pierre Champion is both good-humoured and disillusioned. His voice is musical and far-away. He is for ever dreaming. He does not live among his contemporaries, but with the shades of the past. He almost always wraps himself up in a huge muffler, doubtless lest he should catch cold in the dank shadows of History. As the fifteenth century was his special province, and he had travelled every road, every path and every by-way of it, he used to as-

The Credo of a Sceptic

sist Anatole France in re-reading the proofs of *Jeanne d'Arc*.

"Well," he asked, "when is it going to appear?"

FRANCE.—*I should like it to be soon. But, as you know, my dear friend, I have latterly been greatly delayed by liver troubles, and I am afraid I shall be interrupted again.*

Then Jean Jacques Brousson, his secretary, inquired in tones of filial anxiety:

"Are you still suffering?"

FRANCE.—*No, not suffering, but uneasy. You know how this trouble interferes with work, for you have had it yourself. In fact, that is why you are sorry for me, for one pities oneself through other people.*

BROUSSON.—"Not at all, my dear Master. I do not pity you. It is only just, if Dame Nature tortures your body a little, after having lavished the treasures of the mind upon you."

FRANCE.—*Really?*

BROUSSON.—"If I had your genius, I would gladly suffer the most cruel infirmities."

FRANCE.—*This child does not know what he is saying.*

CHAMPION.—"All the same, there is some sense in his remarks. But, to return to your *Jeanne d'Arc*, I am longing to applaud its success."

FRANCE.—*Your friendship is deceiving you.*

[69]

The Opinions of Anatole France

People will not like my book. No, I assure you, they will not like it. They will not find in it what they are looking for. Oh, I can easily guess what is expected of me: a narrative packed with unctuous indecencies. People will be disappointed. I ought, for instance, to have insisted upon the virginity of my heroine, on the tests to which she was submitted, on the examination made by the matrons appointed by the judges for that purpose. But, I did not, although the temptation to do so was strong. Amongst the documents in the case for her rehabilitation there are some delicious statements concerning the chastity of the Maid.

The captains who were her comrades in arms, and who slept beside her on the straw in the camp, called heaven to witness that no carnal desire ever touched them. They are naïvely astonished to admit it. They, who made it a point of honor always to display their gallantry to the fair sex, are flabbergasted by their reserve towards the saintly maiden. In her presence, as they put it, their senses were stilled. For them that is the most surprising of miracles and the manifest sign of divine intervention.

HYACINTHE LOYSON.[1]—"So it seems to you certain, Master, that she preserved her virtue?"

FRANCE.—*There is really not the slightest*

---

[1] Hyacinthe Loyson who died recently, was the son of the celebrated Modernist.

doubt about it. The matrons of Poitiers brought positive testimony in her favour, though, in this connection, Solomon prudently advises the wise man to reserve judgment. Moreover, you must remember that this virtue, preserved in the midst of the worst blackguards, was a great subject of amazement to her contemporaries. The slightest weakness would immediately have been trumpeted abroad.

Finally, when Jeanne was in the hands of the English she happened to fall ill, and the doctors who attended to her certainly did not fail to verify a matter in which all the judges were interested. If the examination had turned to her discredit, her accusers, according to the ideas of the time, could legitimately have declared her a witch, and possessed by the devil. The strategy of Beelzebub was, in effect, simple and infallible. If he wished to dominate a woman, he began by depriving her of the essential. After that first sacrifice, it seems, she could no longer refuse him anything. She became his most devoted slave. And there was an element of truth in that superstition, for women blindly obey the man who arouses their senses.

LOYSON.—"But what, in the last analysis, what do you think of Jeanne, dear Master?"

FRANCE.—*That she was a valiant girl, very devoted to her king. I am filled with enthusiasm for her bravery, and with horror of the awful bar-*

[71]

barity of the theologians who sent her to the stake.

DREYFOUS [2] "Then you entirely share the feelings of Michelet?"

FRANCE.—*Why not?*

DREYFOUS.—"You are not in love with Jeanne, I suppose? Michelet used to dream about her. He used to see and hear her. Those visions did not surprise him in the least. He himself used to see her in visions. For instance, here is a fact of which I was a witness:

"One day, when I happened to be in Rouen, I saw old Michelet sitting on a milestone at the foot of the great tower in which Jeanne had been captive. I went up to greet him, when suddenly I noticed that his eyes were filled with tears.

" 'What in the world is wrong?' I asked deeply moved.

" 'She is in there,' he replied, pointing to the tower.

"Then, as if he had suddenly awakened:

" 'Oh, I beg your pardon, my friend, I do not know what I am thinking of.' "

FRANCE.—*I like that story, for it is absolutely like dear old Michelet. In order to write history he preferred to proceed by means of hallucinations.*

CHAMPION.—"A lovely epigram!"

[2] Dreyfous, since dead, was a celebrated member of the École des Chartes.

The Credo of a Sceptic

Loyson led our host back to the subject.

"Frankly," he asked, "do the Voices not interfere with your admiration for Jeanne?"

FRANCE.—*Not at all.*

LOYSON.—"What! Do her visions not seem mad to you?"

FRANCE.—*Come, my friend! We all have them.*

LOYSON (astonished)—"How do you mean?"

FRANCE.—*Do you want contemporary instances? Remember the Dreyfus Affair. Our friend Francis de Pressensé at that time used continually to invoke Justice and Truth. He talked of them as of living beings. I am sure he used to see them. And did not Zola proclaim that "Truth was on the March"? He also beheld it as a real person. It appeared to him, I fancy, in the form of a beautiful, dark woman, with a serious face. Probably she looked like Madame Segond-Weber. She was clothed in a white peplum, like the actresses of the Comédie Française when they represent the goddesses of antiquity, and she held well aloft a glittering mirror.*

No. I am wrong. Zola's Truth must have been more naturalistic. Perhaps she reminded him of Mouquette showing . . . you know what! At all events, he used to see her as I see you. Yet, I ask you, my friend. Do Justice and Truth exist?

LOYSON.—"No, obviously. Not in flesh and blood. But they exist."

The Opinions of Anatole France

FRANCE.—*Hello! Now you are becoming a visionary. Justice and Truth, my dear Loyson, exist only in so far as men desire them. And the desire for them is lukewarm. But if Pressensé and Zola allow themselves to be guided by imaginary divinities, are we to laugh at Jeanne because of her Saints, male and female, and her whole heavenly militia?*

Loyson was opening his mouth to protest, but France added immediately:

You will say that she saw ten million angels around her, and that is a lot. It is certainly more than Pressensé and Zola ever saw. But, after all, why quarrel about figures?

We began to laugh.

France continued:

All minds in the fifteenth century were haunted by chimeras. If little Jeanne "saw her Voices," as she naïvely expressed it, her judges, who tried to convict her of sorcery, believed with all their might in demons. But, whereas little Jeanne's dreams were radiant, and impelled her to the most noble enterprises, those of her tormenters were filthy, infamous and monstrous.

However, do not be alarmed, my dear Loyson. If I defend and admire the visions of the poor little herdsmaid, it does not follow that, in writing her history, I have myself given credence to the miracles.

[74]

The Credo of a Sceptic

Quite the contrary. I constantly remembered that it is the duty of the scientist to find a rational explanation for all facts. And I tried to bring out clearly what made Jeanne's mission logically possible.

First and foremost, it was the general credulity of the period. Her position with the Armagnacs was strengthened by the prophecies of Merlin and the Venerable Bede concerning a Maid who would deliver the kingdom. To the troops of the Dauphin and the soldiery of the militia Jeanne was a mascot, whose mere presence aroused their fanaticism, made them oblivious of danger, and gave them victory. On the other hand, her reputation as a sorceress inspired terrible fear in the English, who had hitherto been so greatly dreaded by the people of France, and who were commonly called "Les Coués," that is, the tailed devils. In fact, it was believed that they had little tails behind.

All Jeanne's power, which was undoubtedly considerable, came from the ascendant which she unwittingly established over the feeble mentality of her contemporaries. To this must be added the heroism which the excellent girl displayed on every occasion. When her marvellous adventure is minutely analysed, it arouses the same surprise as a very brilliant star seen through the most powerful astronomical glasses. However greatly it be mag-

nified, the heavenly body always remains a point without diameter.

Jeanne was but little in herself, but the legend which formed about her immediately was splendid, and it has not lost any of its splendour. It must be added that her mission was perhaps easier than one would think, for the English were exhausted and few in numbers. Nor must we forget the skill of Charles VII and his counsellors, for I am quite persuaded that, if he was far from warlike, Charles VII was at least a very shrewd negotiator, who got more by gentle methods from the burghers of the towns than by force, and relied more upon diplomacy than upon arms, one of those good kings, in brief, whose prudence, skill, and tenacity in council, made ancient France great.

CHAMPION (in very gentle tones)—"Never fear, dear Master, you will be blamed for having given a human explanation of this pious story, and for having freed it from *charisms*, to use the theological term. I can already hear your usual opponents. They will say that your sceptical hands should not have touched this sacred image."

FRANCE (with sudden vivacity)—*Sceptic! Sceptic! It is true, they will still call me a sceptic. And for them that is the worst insult. But for me it is the finest praise. A Sceptic! Why, that is what all the masters of French thought have been. Rabelais,*

The Credo of a Sceptic

Montaigne, Molière, Voltaire, Renan—Sceptics.
All the loftiest minds of our race were sceptics, all
those whom I tremblingly venerate, and whose most
humble pupil I am.

At this moment France's voice had lost its customary indolence. It had suddenly become vibrant,
and his usually malicious expression was now tense
and excited.

He continued:

Scepticism! This word is made synonomous
with negation and impotence. Yet, our great
sceptics were sometimes the most affirmative, and
often the most courageous, of men. They denied
only negations. They attacked everything that
fetters the mind and the will. They struggled
against ignorance that stupefies, against error that
oppresses, against intolerance that tyrannizes,
against cruelty that tortures, and against hatred
that kills. They are accused of having been unbe-
lievers. But first we must know whether belief is
a virtue, and whether genuine strength does not lie
in doubting what there is no reason to believe. It
would not be difficult to prove that those Frenchmen
of genius who are called sceptics professed the most
magnificent credo. Each one of them formulated
some article of it.

Rabelais, a buffoon full of seriousness, proclaims
the majesty of tolerance. Like him the Pyrrhonic

The Opinions of Anatole France

Montaigne prostrates himself devoutly before the wisdom of the ancients. Forgetting the oscillations of his doubting mind he invokes pity against the ferocity of religious wars and the barbarity of judicial torture. Above all, he pays homage to the sanctity of friendship. Molière inveighs against the passions and weaknesses which make men hateful, and he preaches the beautiful gospel of sociability. In his wildest capers the unbelieving Voltaire never loses sight of his ideal of reason, knowledge and kindness—yes, kindness, for this great satirist was unkind only to the wicked and the foolish. Finally, Renan always remained a priest; all he did was to purify religion. He believed in the divine, in learning; he believed in the future of mankind. Thus all our sceptics were full of ardour, all strove to deliver their fellow-men from the chains that drag them down. In their own way they were saints.

Some one said: "*Saint Renan,* is the title of one of the chapters of *Souvenirs d'enfance et de jeunesse.*" But none had ever spoken before of Saint Voltaire and Saint Rabelais.

Ignoring the sarcasm, France continued:

People reproach these giants with having presumed too much upon human reason. For my part, I have no excessive confidence in reason. I know how weak and tottering it is. But I remember Diderot's clever apologue: "I have," he said,

The Credo of a Sceptic

*"only a small flickering light to guide me in the
darkness of a thick forest. Up comes a theologian
and blows it out."* Let us first of all follow reason,
it is the surest guide. It warns us itself of its
feebleness and informs us of its own limitations.
Moreover, so far from being incompatible with sen-
timent, it leads to feeling. When we have brooded
deeply, the most sceptical thinkers are seized with
a profound commiseration for their fellow-men, in
the face of the useless and eternal flux of the Universe, of the insignificance of wretched mankind,
and of the absurd suffering which men inflict upon
one another during the brief dream of existence.
It is but a step from that compassion to fraternal
love, and it is easily taken. Pity becomes active,
and he who believed himself to be for ever aloof
from all things jumps desperately into the struggle
to save his unhappy fellow-men. That, my friends,
is how sceptics feel.*

We had listened in silence to this passionate con-
fession of faith. Then France resumed, almost
apologetically:

*No doubt, you will think I have let my feelings
get the better of me. . . . But, the poor sceptics
are really too greatly misunderstood. As a matter
of fact, they are the most idealistic of mortals, but
they are disappointed idealists. Because they
dream of a very beautiful world, they are depressed*

[79]

The Opinions of Anatole France

*at seeing mankind so different from what it ought
to be.   The irony which they affect is merely an
expression of their discouragement.   They laugh,
but their gaiety always conceals a terrible bitterness.   They laugh in order not to weep.*

Here Pierre Champion interjected rather mockingly:

"If Jeanne d' Arc had been a sceptic of the right
school, who knows?   Perhaps she would have accomplished out of love for humanity the magnan-
imous actions which faith inspired in her."

Certainly she would not, replied France smiling,
*for it is only the visionaries who do very great
things.   But observe, oh malicious Pierre Champion, that Voltaire, the most irreligious of men,
also knew how to be brave, when, in defiance of all
the ecclesiastical and judicial powers, he pursued
the rehabilitation of Colas, of Sirven, of the Che-
valier de la Barre, and of Lally-Tollendal.   Do not
forget that, if he sinned in writing "La Pucelle,"
this scoundrel was the first to demand that altars
be raised to Jeanne d'Arc.*[3]   *Rmember also that, if*

[3] *Anatole France is alluding to this sentence in 'l'Histoire
Universelle":*

*"Finally, accused of having dressed again in men's clothes,
which were left purposely to tempt her, these judges, who had
certainly no right to try her since she was a prisoner of war,
declared her an impenitent heretic and burned by slow fire her who,
having saved her King, would have had altars raised to her in the
heroic age, when men paid such honour to their liberators."*

The Credo of a Sceptic

the judges of Jeanne d' Arc had been sceptical philosophers, instead of pious fanatics, they would certainly never have burned her. The conclusion is,
my dear friend, that scepticism prompts the most
humane sentiments, and that, in any case, it pre-
vents crimes.

I have recited my Credo. Amen!

Professor Brown and the Secret
of Genius

Professor Brown and the Secret of Genius

Wrapped in his beige dressing-gown with brown stripes, and with his eternal little crimson skull-cap on his head, France was seated at his writing-table turning over the pages of a very old book bound in pigskin. A soft and variegated light fell upon the writer from the window ornamented with those knobs of glass, set in lead, which the master glaziers call *sives*. It looked like a Rembrandt picture of some philosopher meditating in an attic, or rather, some Doctor Faustus consulting the Cabala.

Our host stood up to receive us.

You are wondering what is this venerable tome. It is "La Chronologie collé." I was looking in it for a portrait of Rabelais.

He turned a few pages.

Look. Here it is. It was engraved by Léonard Gaultier some fifty years after the death of the great satirist. We do not possess one engraved during his lifetime, and this little picture is the oldest in which his features are recorded. Moreover, it is possibly like him.[1] What do you think of it.

[1] *In point of fact, L'Estoile, who bought "La Chronologie collé" when it appeared in 1601, wrote this criticism at the head*

The Opinions of Anatole France

Remy de Gourmont,[2] who was present, looked at the vignette and said:

"What a harsh expression! A real Bogey Man! His forehead is marked with deep wrinkles, and the veins stand out as thick as ropes. His sunken eyes gleam with a sombre ardour. One would

of the Rabelais portrait: "which in no wise resembleth him." In this fashion he bore witness against the resemblance of this portrait.—See Clouzot, Les Portraits de Rabelais, Gazette des Beaux Arts, 1911. But perhaps the legend which had already formed about Master Alcofribas had substituted in the mind of L'Estoile the conventional type of a genial buffoon for the recollection of the grave personage whom he had known a long time before.

[2] Remy de Gourmont liked to call on Anatole France. When these two rare and charming minds came into contact they gave out sparks like flint and iron, and it was a heavenly delight to hear them. Remy de Gourmont was paradox personified, but often more sensible paradox than vulgar good sense. He was all feeling, but a hideous cancer which disfigured his face isolated him in the torture of a tenderness he could never express. Out of spite he was often ironical, and sometimes even at the expense of love.

That morning I had met him in the Avenue du Bois de Boulogne, before he had reached France's house. For a moment we watched together some doves of variegated hue, as they billed and cooed on the grass. Suddenly he began:

"The Ancients gave doves in homage to Venus, because they are very voluptuous. But they were mistaken. There are more amorous creatures."

.. 'What are they?' "I asked attentively.

"Snails!"

I gave a shiver of disgust and incredulity.

"Yes," he continued, "snails. The zoologists tell us, in effect, that Dame Nature, full of generosity towards these little beasts, has overwhelmed them with joy, by giving them each the attributes of both the male and the female. And when snails come together each little horned creature experiences a double pleasure.

Professor Brown

surely expect more joviality in the Priest of Meudon. As Ronsard says:

> Jamais le soleil ne l'a veu,
> Tant fust-il matin, qu'il n'eust beu.
> Et jamais, au soir, la nuit noire,
> Tant fust tard, ne l'a veu sans boire.
>
> .   .   .   .
>
> Il se couchait tout plat à bas
> Sur la jonchée, entre les taces;
> Et parmi les escuelles grasses
> Sans nulle honte se souillant
> Comme une grenouille en la fange. . . .

"But that Bacchic epitaph must lie, for 'Gargantua' and 'Pantagruel' are not at all comic. Léonard Gualtier is right."

FRANCE.—*I picture him as you do. Rabelais is not the boon companion one imagines. His expressions and locutions are coarse and strong, but his ideas are thoughtful. He delivers austere homilies. In short, his gaiety is merely on the surface, and his laugh ill conceals his profound seriousness.*

His gloomy look is not surprising, said one of us, since he was a scholar.

FRANCE.—*I beg your pardon. Rabelais was not*

Each is simultaneously lover and mistress.
"It is a pity these animals move so slowly for they deserve more than doves to drag the chariot of Cypris."
It was with such merry discourse that he beguiled our way to the door of M. Bergeret.

[87]

The Opinions of Anatole France

what we call a scholar, for he is never a bore. He is not joyful, but he never tires. He happened to bring out an edition of the Aphorisms of Hippocrates, but he omitted to preserve the manuscript commentaries. Why? Probably because he did not find them interesting.

Now, what is a scholar? A deadly creature who studies and publishes on principle everything that is fundamentally uninteresting. So, Rabelais is not a scholar. Yet, he had pretty solid erudition, it cannot be denied. And for a man whose learning was the least of his virtues, his was rather pleasing. Do not certain of his fanatical admirers credit him with omniscience? For example, in connection with the military operations of Gargantua against Pichrochole, they declare that Rabelais is a great strategist. But, that is a joke. On that principle, any writer would be a consummate tactician. Any time you like I bet I could write a booklet of one hundred and fifty pages on "Paul de Kock: Tactician." I would go to "Le Cocu" for my material. In that novel there is an old soldier who trains a parrot to cry: "Port arms! Present arms! Shoulder arms . . . epp! etc." I would write a gloss on that.

"Notice," I would say, "what a wonderful soldier this Paul de Kock was. He is thoroughly familiar with the arts of war. 'Port arms!' is, in fact, the

command given to a soldier when he is to raise his rifle."

I would continue:

"We have collated this passage with a military manual of 1830, and on page 25, paragraph 3, we found the command: 'Port arms!' This movement is composed as follows: 'Raise the rifle with the right hand to the level of the shoulder, grasp it in the left hand, etc. . . .'"

In this fashion I would exploit the psittacism of the learned bird. Conclusion: In tactics Paul de Kock could have given lessons to Napoleon the First. And so the trick is done.

The truth is, Master Alcofribas was not more deeply versed than Paul de Kock in the arts of war. Has not somebody discovered in Gargantua references to the wars of François I and Charles V? Pure nonsense! The workings of the imagination of Rabelais have been reconstructed. He was not at all inspired by the great events of his time, but, on the contrary, by very insignificant facts whose memory had remained with him from youth. Some of the proper names which he uses are those of people he had known. I do not guarantee, how-ever, that he got those of Humevesne and Baisecul from real life. But the episode itself of these two advocates was suggested to him by a lawsuit in which he was involved.

[89]

The Opinions of Anatole France

*In the same way, the differences of Grandgousier
and Pichrochole represent quarrels which had set
the peasants of Touraine at loggerheads, and whose
grotesque echoes had amused him. No doubt he
wished to imply that the wars of the proudest sovereigns were astonishingly like the brawls of yokels—
a truth with a fine flavour of irony!*

*No, my friends, Rabelais was not a great strate-
gist. He was quite satisfied to be a great writer.*

. . . .

Joséphine showed in Mr. Brown, Professor of
Philology at the University of Sydney.

He is a stout, robust man, with a brick-red complexion, and clean-shaven upper lip and chin. His
powerful muscles are a proof of his assiduous cult
of golf and polo. He wears gold spectacles. His
red hair, brushed down in front, is as stiff as the
bristles of a boar.

We were struck by his Anglo-Saxon elegance.

Seen at close hand his suit was a coarse-grained
tweed, showing every colour in the rainbow, but
from a distance it assumed the greenish, indefinite
colour of split-pea soup. A small red tie, which
affected an air of conquest, was attached to his soft
collar, from which his bull neck emerged. Tan
shoes, as long and as broad as a steamboat, com-
pleted the dress of this solid and learned Australian.

FRANCE.—*What can I do for you, Professor?*

Professor Brown

Mr. Brown, expressing himself in French with extreme difficulty, and furthermore embarrassed by an attack of shyness which seized him in the presence of a celebrated man, stammered as best he could:

"Je . . . vô . . . je voulais voir vô."

FRANCE.—*I am deeply honoured, Sir, and the pleasure is mutual. Won't you take a seat, and satisfy your wish.*

When Mr. Brown had sat down he continued, halting after each word: "I was looking for . . . I wanted to know the mystery . . . the secret of literary genius. . . ."

FRANCE.—*If I understood you rightly, you are preparing a thesis on literary genius.*

"Yes!" shouted Professor Brown, radiant at having been understood. "Yes, yes."

FRANCE.—*Well, just as you came in our conversation, by a happy coincidence, turned upon one of the greatest geniuses of France and of the whole world, Rabelais.*

"Yes. Rabelais. Yes."

Mr. Brown's eyes beamed with joy.

FRANCE.—*What is the secret of his genius? You ask me a thorny question. By what qualities did he surpass other writers?*

Has it not been said that he wrote badly? some one objected.

The Opinions of Anatole France

FRANCE.—*All great authors write badly. That is well known. At least, the pedants say so. Great writers are impetuous. The vigour of their vocabulary, the intensity of their style, the daring of their phrases, disconcert the pedants. To the pundits good writing apparently means writing according to rules. But born writers make their own rules, or rather make none. They change their manner at every moment, as inspiration dictates, sometimes they are harmonious, sometimes rugged, sometimes indolent and sometimes spirited. So, according to the common notion, they cannot write well. And why deny it? Rabelais is not free from faults. His litanies of nouns, his strings of epithets, his lines of verbs, undoubtedly prove his inexhaustible imagination, but they make his style heavy. His phrases often lack suppleness, cadence and balance.*

It would not be difficult to find in the old authors more regularity, clarity and harmony. "Le Ménagier," for instance, which was written long before Gargantua, contains some lovely passages about bread, wine and bees. No doubt the old language creates an illusion, for distance gives an exquisite shade to the things of the past, and we find charm in what had but little for men of an earlier age. Yet, I do not think I am mistaken. "Le Ménagier" is charmingly written. It would be good Rabelais, if it were Rabelais. . . . That is, if it did not

Professor Brown

lack genius. Similarly, the "Contes" of the Seigneur des Accords are full of charm. His style flows and is a delight to the ear. It is better than that of Rabelais. Nevertheless, it is Rabelais who is the great writer, and not the Seigneur des Accords.

One of us suggested: Molière also writes badly.

FRANCE.—*Yes, indeed, Molière also writes badly, And so do Saint-Simon, and Balzac and all the others, I tell you! In Molière's time certain writers, Saint-Evremond and Furetière, for example, used a much more polished syntax. They were purer. Only, Molière is Molière, that is to say, not a good, but a great writer.*

Professor Brown Still Searches

Professor Brown Still Searches

Professor Brown did not lose a word of the discourse. He was listening with his ears, of course, but also with his wide open eyes, and above all, with his gaping mouth. Suddenly he plunged bravely into the stream of talk.

"I . . . always thought . . . that the great . . . writers were those . . . who worked hardest."

We had all followed his stammering words with anxious politeness.

With the utmost courtesy France asked him:

Perhaps you are thinking, Professor, of the famous adage of Buffon: "Genius is a long patience."

"Ah!" said the Australian emphatically, his eyes swimming with infinite gratitude.

FRANCE.—*Well, I strongly suspect that this sentence is untrue.*

Mr. Brown's features were veiled in sadness, but he opened his mouth more eagerly than ever.

FRANCE.—*Yes, that maxim is false. Geniuses are not the most painstaking of men. Or rather, there is no hard-and-fast rule. Some men of genius, I grant, are very diligent. Our Flaubert is one of*

The Opinions of Anatole France

them.[1] *He tried a hundred phrases in order to write one. And Dumas fils very justly said of him: "He is a cabinet-maker who cuts down a whole forest to make a wardrobe." But other geniuses are careless to excess, and this kind is perhaps the least rare. In Rabelais, to return to that subject, many careless slips are noticeable. He consecrated to his work, as he has told us himself, "only such time as was devoted to the needs of the body, to wit, while eating and drinking."*

He did not write; he dictated, and he gave rein to his imagination. Consequently, the dimensions of his giants vary continually. Sometimes they are taller than the towers of Notre-Dame, sometimes they scarcely exceed human measurements. At the end of the second book he announces that Panurge is going to marry and that his wife will make a cuckold of him in the first month of their wedded life, that Pantagruel will find the Philosopher's Stone, and that he will wed the daughter of John the priest, King of India. But not one of these things happens in the following books. Rabelais completely forgot his fine programme. In short, he was the most careless of geniuses.

REMY DE GOURMONT.—"Oh, well! The greatest

[1] *Anatole France is also. It is therefore all the greater merit in him that he should recognise the beauty of improvisation in others.*

Spanish writer, Cervantes, was probably even less careful. His thoughtlessness betrays him everywhere. The day after Don Quixote leaves his house, his housekeeper tells the priest he has been gone a week. Sancho bewails the loss of his ass which has been stolen from him by the thief, Ginés de Pasamonte, and a few pages further on he remounts his beast which has inexplicably returned. Sancho's wife is first called Joan and then Teresa. And, strangest of all, the corpulent attendant of the Knight of la Mancha is not shown at the outset as he appears in the course of the story. It is only after several chapters, for example, that the author attributes to him the pleasant mania for breaking out into proverbs. Many passages of the masterpiece of Saavedra show striking signs of hasty work."

FRANCE.—*What did I tell you, Professor! And coming to one of your own geniuses, could not Shakespeare, too, be caught in the very act of carelessness? For instance, he says repeatedly that the witches made three prophecies to Macbeth. In truth, they greet him with three titles, Thane of Glamis, Thane of Cawdor and King. But, as Macbeth was already Thane of Glamis when they appeared to him, there were only two prophecies, not three, with all due respect to the great Will. I*

The Opinions of Anatole France

will not dwell on the port of Bohemia, on the clock which strikes the hour, in ancient Rome, and on many other charming points which you know.

Ignorance or carelessness? In any case you can see, what a free-and-easy fashion geniuses botch their sublime works. Whatever may be said, patience is the least of their virtues. They take no pains. They are great as beautiful women are beautiful—without effort. That idea, I admit, clashes somewhat with current morality. People would like to think that glory is achieved at the cost of some labour. When geniuses are presented as models to young people, the latter are usually told: "Work hard! Grind away! and you will be like them." And that, indeed would be more just. But then, what does nature care for justice! Mediocrities sweat blood only to produce rubbish. Geniuses create wonders without an effort. In short, it is much easier to produce a masterpiece than a rhapsody, for all things are easy . . . to the predestined mortal.

. . . .

Mr. Brown seemed to be overwhelmed. He persisted, however, in his inquiry.

"Then, Monsieur France, do you not think that the chief quality of the great writers is beauty of imagination?"

FRANCE.—*Wealth of imagination?*

Professor Brown Still Searches

MR. BROWN.—"Oh!"

FRANCE.—*Perhaps.*

REMY DE GOURMONT.—"Indeed, nothing is less certain. Almost all celebrated authors, on the contrary, have cut their finest garments from pieces of cloth which other hands have woven. As Molière put it, they took their material where they found it. The more one reads Rabelais, Molière and La Fontaine, to•mention only these, the more the share of their own inventiveness diminishes."

FRANCE.—*Very true, my dear friend. The raw material rarely belongs to them. They borrow it, and simply give it a new turn. Nowadays there is a rage for skinning geniuses. It is a fashionable pastime. People look for the sources of their works. Their detractors denounce their plagiarisms. Their devotees do the same, but they are careful to say that, when the peacock subtracts some blue feathers from the jackdaw to mix with the eyes of its tail, the jackdaw has no reason to complain, because the peacock has done it a great honour. And when the opponents and the devotees of a cult have struggled for some twenty years over an idol, it would seem as if nothing remains but dust. What survives of Rabelais after the researches of the Rabelaisians, and of Cervantes after those of his adorers, and of Molière after those of the Molièrists? In truth, I believe they remain what they*

The Opinions of Anatole France

always were, that is, very great men. But modern criticism, by showing us where they went to find each little stone of their mosaic, might end by persuading us that their reputation is undeserved. So far as Rabelais is concerned, for instance, nothing more belongs to him. They say, this page is Tory, that is Lucian, this is from Thomas More, and that from Colonna.

It is all true. What is more, Rabelais actually seems less intelligent than the authors from whom he derives his inspiration, yes, less intelligent. Compare the episode of the Limousin Scholar in Tory and in Pantagruel. I will briefly summarize it. The good giant Pantagruel meets a young coxcomb who boasts that he is studying in Paris, and who speaks a French strangely embellished with Latin. To express the fact that he is in the habit of crossing the Seine morning and evening, he says:

"Nous transfretons la Séquane au dilicule et au crépuscule."

And in a mood for gallant confidences he relates that the Parisian students like to "inculquer leurs vérètres ès pudendes de mérétricules amicabilissimes, etc . . . etc. . . ."

Pantagruel listens to him for some time in astonishment. Then, suddenly losing patience, he seizes him by the throat and shakes him like a puppy. Then the student, in his terror, spoils his

[102]

Professor Brown Still Searches

breeches and begins to beg for mercy in the patois of Limoges. That is the story.

Now, Tory begins by explaining why his character speaks Latin first. It is because this provincial does not know French. The only living tongue he has mastered is his local dialect, and if he has recourse to Latin it is by no means out of affectation, but because Latin was the universal speech, the esperanto of the period. Then suddenly, in a grip of the giant, he returns to his native language, which is that of Limoges.

On the other hand, Rabelais gives no explanation, and consequently his version of the adventure is less comprehensible. But, as he does not set any limit upon our conjectures, we imagine that, if the scholar talks a pedantic jargon, in which there is much less French than Latin, it is to increase his own importance, to flabbergast Pantagruel. And we laugh heartily when, under pressure of fear, this stupid pedant reveals all of a sudden his humble origin by his provincial gibberish. Thus he marvellously symbolizes the pretentious hollowness of the pseudo-educated who have the gift of the gab. And in that way the story, though not so well constructed, takes on a much wider significance.

Similarly, compare the "Icaromenippus" of Lucian with the episode of the woodcutter Couillatris in the prologue to the Fourth Book of Pantagruel.

The Opinions of Anatole France

You will see that Rabelais appears less intelligent than Lucian. In the "Icaromenippus" Jupiter, having opened a little trap-door at the foot of his throne, leans over it to listen attentively to the prayers of mortals. Filled with a sense of equity, the father of gods and men puts carefully aside the reasonable requests, in order to grant them, and he blows furiously upon the swarm of unjust prayers, in order to drive them away from him.

The Jupiter of Rabelais, on the contrary, follows no method. As the appalling din of the supplications rising from the whole universe is head-splitting, he completely loses his wits. He muddles everything, and it is a matter of mere chance whether he showers benefactions upon men, or overwhelms them with misfortunes. Yet, observe that, in this extravagant form, the buffoonery borders on the sublime. With Lucian it was a rhetorical elaboration. With our Rabelais it is a profound satire on the blindness of Destiny.

That is the way great men make mistakes. Whatever they may do, they are always right, because what they invent is not the result of cold calculation, but of a powerful natural instinct. They create just as mothers bring children into the world. All the statues they model have the breath of life, though they know not why. Even though their statues be twisted and deformed, they are alive, they

Professor Brown Still Searches

are not still-born, whereas those modelled by other sculptors according to the rules are dead.

. . . .

Mr. Brown was more and more discouraged, because he did not succeed in discovering why men of genius are superior to vulgar mortals. Every time he thought he had lit upon a point of superiority it vanished under analysis. With the energy of despair, he managed to stutter:

"If the great writers . . . do not imagine the things themselves . . . they write them better, perhaps. . . ."

FRANCE.—*You say that they have the merit of composing well.*

Frankly, Professor, I think that you are deceiving yourself in this. I know, of course, that composition usually is regarded as the primary condition of the art of writing. It is one of those eternal verities which our respectable university teaches its offspring as inalterable dogmas. No salvation without plan! Such is the doctrine. Literary work is regarded as a sort of theorem whose propositions are mutually determined, follow one another, and hasten towards the Q. E. D. But nothing of the kind is visible in the work of many geniuses. Rabelais, Cervantes and Swift troubled very little about the construction of their novels.

It is only too clear that Master Alcofribas had

The Opinions of Anatole France

*not the slightest idea of what he was driving at.
When he began "Pantagruel" there is no doubt that
he did not know exactly what he was going to put
into it. The episodes happen without any order,
and all are perfect. What more is needed? It is
a capricious and heavenly excursion.*

*Panurge wants to take unto himself a wife, but
he is deeply afraid that he will be made a cuckold.
Thereupon he consults the wise men and the fools.
Then he sets off to consult the Oracle of the Bottle,
and we embark with him upon the dark blue sea,
zigzagging our course from shore to shore. All
the time adventures are related which have nothing
whatever to do with the gnawing anxiety of Panurge. Where is the plan in all that?*

*The finest masterpieces are made in compart-
ments, into which the writer puts whatever he likes.
They expand, swell out and distend as they are
made. Encouraged by the success of his first book
the author continues.*

*That is what happened with "Pantagruel" and
also with "Don Quixote," of which Gourmont was
talking a moment ago. Like Rabelais, Cervantes
follows only his own fancy. He advances, retraces
his steps, runs, stops, rests in the fields and plunges
into the woods. Now he is amongst the shepherds,
now amongst the nobility, now amongst brigands.
He has no goal. He showed such indifference in*

Professor Brown Still Searches

his "Don Quixote" that any other man would assuredly have lost, but he won. Some have that privilege.

Theoretically, the interest of his narrative should decrease. In point of fact, the first form of humour exploited by Cervantes is by far the most amusing, in principle, at least. In the beginning of the book, it is the sheer madness of the hero that provokes laughter. He is only his own victim. He is the dupe of his own crazy imagination, which causes him to mistake windmills for giants and a flock of sheep for an army. Further on, however, he has almost recovered his reason, and it is no longer he who creates his own misfortunes. It is idle noblemen who play him a thousand scurvy tricks. They drive him mad with all sorts of fireworks. They plant him blindfolded upon a wooden horse which they shake, and persuade him that he is riding through the air. They throw into his room wild cats that claw his face. In short, they work up every conceivable kind of practical joke against him. It might be feared that the disapproval which these tricks arouse would detract from their humour. Not at all. This fine novel holds one with increasing interest to the last page. It is nothing short of a miracle.

REMY DE GOURMONT.—"But is it not the supreme skill of the good authors, that they can

The Opinions of Anatole France

follow indolently their own caprices which guide them so well?"

FRANCE.—*My dear friend, everything is charming in the writers we love. For them we make infinite allowances, and we praise them for what we condemn in others. As we have decided beforehand that they are excellent, they always appear so to us.*

Listen. One day a rather amusing experience happened to me.

I had given the manuscript of a novel to a newspaper. As I was going away, I had divided the sheets into sections, each representing an instalment.

These sections had been placed in a rack with a lot of pigeon holes, in several rows. As luck would have it, the compositor made a mistake. He took the copy from the pigeonholes vertically, instead of from left to right, as he ought to have done. My story had neither beginning nor end, but nobody noticed it. I was even complimented by certain discriminating critics on the delightful whims of my imagination. I was touched by their fervour.

I am sure, my dear Gourmont, that you have far more legitimate reasons for admiring the disorder of Rabelais and Cervantes. What, after all, does it matter where they lead us? Are we not only too happy to dawdle with them in the thousand flowery halting-places along the road? The

Professor Brown Still Searches

very disconnectedness of their plots is an imitation of the surprises of life. It is like the succession of day following day. And then, it must be admitted, a more robust unity is visible in their works than that of a well connected plot. That is, the cohesion of their spirit. The episodes are scattered, but the thought which plays all through them is always clear and well defined. It is a beautiful, internal radiance which illuminates, vivifies and harmonizes the most varied adventures.

What nobility, what pride, in "Don Quixote," for example! What amiable sarcasm! What lofty poetry! What kindness! The more to appreciate these rare merits one must read Avellaneda's insipid imitation. This Spaniard, you know, a contemporary of Cervantes, had the impertinence to write a sequel to "Don Quixote," in order to deprive the author of part of his glory and profit. Cervantes revolted, and he was right, for during his lifetime this plagiarism must have injured him. But nowadays I would like the uninspired elucubration of the imitator to be published in the same edition as the masterpiece. The caricature would enhance the beauty of the original.

It so happens that, while Cervantes displays all his genius by abandoning himself to his entirely spontaneous humour, the other adopts a plan, and sets before himself a purpose. Avellaneda regards

[109]

The Opinions of Anatole France

his pen merely as an instrument for demonstrating the excellence of the Faith. All his stories tend towards that end. And what stories they are! Judge for yourselves:

Sancho, for instance, meets a beautiful Moorish girl, and in a transport of enthusiasm he cries:

"Would to God that all the fleas in my bed were like this young Mohametan!"

"What Sancho," growls |Don Quixote, "is it you who speak so frivolously, you, the husband of Teresa! Assuredly your spouse is outrageously ugly, but she is a good Christian, Sancho. And our holy Mother, the Church, enjoins you to find her more seductive than the most beautiful Musulman women."

But what Avellaneda especially recommends is devotion to the Rosary. He is never tired of expatiating upon the blessings reserved to the pious who tell their beads assiduously. Amongst the edifying and incongruous homilies which he embroiders upon this theme there is one well known because our Nodier made a story of it. I cannot even understand how that storyteller succeeded in imparting some charm to this feeble invention.

This is the story.

A nun, a young sister whom an elegant gentleman noticed while passing the half-opened door of a convent, corresponded with the seducer and decided to join him. In spite of her guilty passion she had not ceased to show ardent devotion to the Holy Virgin. At the moment when she was about to flee from the convent she was driven by an impulse of her heart to the chapel of Mary. She laid upon the steps of the altar her religious habit which she had taken off to put on secular clothing.

With her lover, as you may imagine, she experienced only disappointment, suffering and torment. That was a foregone conclusion.

After some years, having drunk the cup of bitterness to the dregs, her soul torn with remorse, she passes by her old convent. She re-enters, and goes to the chapel of the Virgin. Behold, a miracle! Her habit is there on the steps of the altar, in the very place where she had left it. She puts it on again. A moment later she meets a young sister who, showing not the slightest astonishment at her return, talks to her as if the lost sheep had never left the fold.

"Sister, the Mother Superior wants the bunch of keys which she gave you this morning."

And the repentant sinner actually finds hanging on her girdle these keys which are wanted.

A sudden light inundates her soul.

All during her long and lamentable adventure the

The Opinions of Anatole France

Holy Virgin, touched by her fervour, and pitying her weakness, assumed her likeness, wore her clothes, and played her part in the convent.

Ah, the great virtues of the Rosary!

Then France, without any warning, turned to Mr. Brown:

Listen, Professor, if you were inspired by devotion, eminent devotion, to the Rosary, at this very moment the Virgin would be giving your lectures in philology at the University of Sydney.

Mr Brown began to roll his frightened, globular eyes behind his gold spectacles.

But, my dear Master, objected Jean Jacques Brousson, France's secretary, there would surely be some difficulty for the Virgin in taking the place of a person of a different sex from her own.

FRANCE.—*You do not understand. Nothing is too difficult for her. If there be great devotion, that suffices. The proof is this other story of Avellaneda.*

A very brave knight was wonderfully devoted to the Rosary. At dawn one holiday he went into the chapel of the Virgin to attend mass. He liked it so much that he wanted to hear a second mass and then a third. After that he remained for a long time absorbed in prayer. Towards the middle of the day he became again conscious of the outer world, and suddenly he remembered that he ought to have gone in the morning to a solemn tournament to measure his prowess against his equals. He had issued a great many challenges. What would people think of his absence? Without a doubt, he had been accused of retreating. His honour was lost!

He comes out of the chapel, and, scarcely has he done so, when he is greeted with frantic applause.

He thinks that people are making fun of him and blushes to the roots of his hair. He struggles against his admirers.

"Leave me alone," he says to them. "Leave me alone. I do not deserve your mockery!"

"Our mockery! Never was an ovation more sincere."

"Stop, I tell you! I will soon have my revenge."

"What revenge do you talk of taking? You, the victor of victors!"

At this moment a powerful fellow, with broken armour, comes forward and says:

"Allow me to shake your hand. One cannot feel any rancour towards so courageous a rival!"

Then the pious knight has no more doubts. A great miracle has happened in his favour.

While he was praying so fervently it was the Virgin, the Virgin herself, who assumed his appearance, mounted his horse, broke many a lance, tumbled nearly a dozen braggarts head over heels in

The Opinions of Anatole France

the sand of the lists, and gathered a magnificent harvest of laurels for her faithful adorer.

Whereupon France turned to his secretary:

For shame, little sceptic!

Then, to the professor from Sydney:

So you see, dear Mr. Brown, it would be child's play for the Holy Virgin to take your place . . . that is, if we are to believe Avellaneda.

MR. BROWN.—But my religion does not authorize the worship of the Virgin.

FRANCE.—*Well, really, Professor! So much the worse for you!*

Professor Brown Bewildered

Professor Brown Bewildered

Professor Brown was not satisfied. He stared at the floor in gloomy silence.

Tell me, Professor, I beg you, asked Anatole France, *whence comes this worried look upon your face?*

MR. BROWN.—"Ah! M. France, I am less advanced now than when I came in, for, if I have understood you aright, great writers have no merit, neither correctness of style, nor the labour which makes perfection, nor imagination, nor method in the arrangement of their stories."

FRANCE.—*Let us be quite clear. Some have those qualities, but many others have not, and yet they are geniuses. That proves they are not indispensable to great writers.*

MR. BROWN. (*energetically*)—"*Then, tell me,* what qualities are indispensable?"

His distress was comic. He looked like a drowning man searching for a buoy in a raging sea.

FRANCE.—*Dear Mr. Brown, what is a quality*

The Opinions of Anatole France

and what is a defect?   We must know that, first of all.

He remained thoughtful for a moment, then addressed us all:

"Yes.   It is true.   These terms are all relative. What seems good to one judge, seems bad to another.   And, above all, what is a quality for one generation becomes a defect for the following.

For example, Brossette makes a curious remark. He reports a judgment upon Malherbe by Despréaux.

"Malherbe," the author of "l'Art Poétique" declared , "was not free from the faults with which he reproached his predecessors.   Thus, one sometimes finds unexpected rhymes in his works."

There is the theory which was current in the great century.   In order to be good, the rhyme had to be foreseen by the reader or the auditor.

Example:

> "Puisque Vénus le veut, de ce sang déplorable
> Je péris la dernière et la plus misérable."

In these two lines of Racine the rhyme seemed excellent to his contemporaries because they expected it: "déplorable" naturally suggested "misérable."   And just for the same reason the rhyme seems bad to us.   But do not forget that certain rhymes in Racine strike us as excellent: this, for example:

Professor Brown Bewildered

"Ah! qu'ils s'aiment, Phénix, j'y consens. Qu'elle parte!
Que charmés l'un de l'autre, ils retournent à Sparte!"

But that was precisely the sort of rhyme his contemporaries thought was bad, because it was unexpected.

We Parnassians, on the other hand, demanded rare and unusual rhymes. We swooned with delight when charming Théodore de Banville invented amusing ones, such as

"... des escaliers
Qu'un Titan, de sa main gigantesque, a liés."

I beg your pardon, Professor. No doubt these remarks on French versification are too subtle to interest you. But I will choose more striking instances to show you that the qualities of yesterday are the defects of today. Let us return to your Shakespeare, if you like.

"Oh!" said Mr. Brown.

FRANCE.—*Juliet says to Romeo:*

"If my kinsmen do see thee, they will murder thee."

Whereupon Romeo replies:

"There lies more peril in thine eyes
Than twenty of their swords."

We call that preciosity, and to us it seems a defect.

Another example:

In "Hamlet" Laertes, weeping for the death of

[119]

his sister, Ophelia, who has just drowned herself, cries piteously:

"Too much of water hast thou, poor Ophelia,
And therefore I forbid my tears."

Instead of moving us, that makes us laugh, does it not?

As you know, the great Will was full of such conceits. We criticize them, for, in our opinion, they are faults of taste. They are blots which unfortunately tarnish the splendour of Shakespeare. But we must remember that all the writers of Elizabeth's court wrote the same way. There was an epidemic of fustian in poetry. Euphuism was triumphant. The rhymers expressed themselves only in affectations. Love, hatred, hope, sorrow, all the passions were put into puzzles and charades.

Referring to Alexander the Great when he had fallen in love, Lyly, the most celebrated of Shakespeare's contemporaries, made the following comment, which he thought was clever:

"A spirit, whose greatness the entire orbit of the world could not contain, is now imprisoned in the narrow orbit of a languishing eye."

Well, when you come to think of it, if mannerisms were the defect of everybody at the time, then they were not really a defect. On the contrary, they were a quality. The more involved, obscure and far-fetched a poet was, the more he was applauded. And the chief merit of Shakespeare in the eyes of the English at this time was precisely that we consider his worst defect.

All the greatest authors are in the same boat. What their contemporaries admired in them is just what displeases us. Dante sometimes tires us with a kind of mumbo-jumbo which he constantly uses. He attributes special virtues to figures. He explains the mysterious influence of the number 9 and its root, 3. He elaborates a system of abstruse symbols, in which the passions are represented by a forest, sensual desire by a panther, pride by a lion and avarice by a she-wolf, while Beatrice Portinari is theology triumphant.

These pretentious obscurities disconcert us. They would spoil Dante for us, if it were possible to spoil him. But then, thirteenth century Scholasticism delighted in such puzzles, and Dante owed almost all his fame to this abuse of riddles.

Similarly, when Rabelais wallows in Greek and Latin, when he piles up references and quotations, he wearies us. In the sixteenth century, however, it was this apparatus of pedantry which particularly delighted the reader. This sauce of antiquity then seemed as necessary to literature as Roman profiles to the monuments of Philibert de L'Orme,

The Opinions of Anatole France

as pagan ruins to the stained-glass windows of Jean Cousin, and the dancing satyrs in the enamels of Penicaud.

But, I see you are pensive, my dear Gourmont.

REMY DE GOURMONT.—"I was thinking that, if the reasons for liking great writers change in this fashion, the traditional admiration shown to them is most mysterious."

FRANCE.—Most mysterious, indeed. After all, if we continue to like them, perhaps it is only because we have got into the habit of doing so.

At this Mr. Brown gave a start. He was scandalized.

"Oh, M. France. Do not say that! Do not say that! I am sure there are qualities in the good authors which always remain qualities, yes, always, always!"

Anatole France gazed ironically at his interrupter, then said slowly, in a conciliatory tone:

Well, may be you are right, Professor.

And he added, looking at Remy de Gourmont:

Yes. No doubt. Don't you think so? After all . . . !

This is a string of phrases which he habitually employs. In a discussion, when he has well weighed the pros and the cons, when he has hesitated for a long time, and when he finally seems to suspend judgment, then he often clings to some probability

Professor Brown Bewildered

suggested by common sense, to some comforting likelihood.

Yes. No doubt. Don't you think so? After all . . . !

That means that the thing is not absolutely certain, but it might be true, and that, in any case, it is better to believe it is.

Yes. No doubt. Don't you think so? After all . . . ! great authors have eternal qualities.

At this point, Mr. Brown's curiosity redoubled, and he opened his mouth wider than ever.

FRANCE.—*If the slightest trifle from their pen enchants us it is because a wise head and a sensitive heart always guide their hand.*

It is a matter of indifference that their syntax is a little shaky, since these very slips are evidence of the powerful drive of the mind which is guilty of the atrocities. It is the syntax of passion.

It is a matter of indifference that they pillage right and left, and that sometimes they get mixed in the plot of their stories. What matters in them is, not the story, however beautifully told, but the opinions and ideas which it clothes. Like nurses rocking babies, they spin us at haphazard adorable stories which go back to the beginning of time. We eagerly swallow the bait, and there is wisdom concealed in the honey of their fables. Thus, in the course of centuries the same anecdotes serve to ex-

The Opinions of Anatole France

press the varying thoughts of the most enlightened men.

All really great men have the prime virtue of, sincerity. They extirpate hypocrisy from their hearts; they bravely reveal their weaknesses, their doubts, their vices. They dissect themselves. They expose their bared souls, so that all their contemporaries may recognize themselves in this picture, and reject the lies which corrupt their lives. They are courageous. They are not afraid to challenge prejudices. No power, civil, moral or immoral, can impose upon them.

Sometimes, it is true, frankness is so dangerous that it would cost them their liberty or even their lives. Under the most liberal, as under the most tyrannical, governments, to proclaim what will be recognized as just and right fifty or a hundred years later is sufficient to incur imprisonment or the scaffold.

As it is better to speak than to be silent, the wise often behave like fools, in order not to be gagged. They gambol, shake their cap and bells, and give utterance to the most reasonable follies. They are allowed to caper because they are taken for buffoons. This stratagem must not be held up against them. Concerning the opinions which he held dearly Rabelais used to say mockingly: "I will maintain them to the stake . . . exclusively." Was he wrong?

[124]

Professor Brown Bewildered

And if he had gone to the stake would it now be possible for us to enjoy his pantagruelism?

Great writers have not mean souls. That, Mr. Brown, is all their secret.

They profoundly love their fellow-men. They are generous—They do not limit their affections. They pity all suffering, and strive to soothe it. They take compassion on the poor players who perform in the comic tragedy, or the tragi-comedy, of destiny. Pity, you see, is the very basis of genius, Professor.

"Oh!" cried Mr. Brown, whose eyes were now shining with joy behind his gold-rimmed spectacles. "Let me shake your hand, M. France." And he inflicted on him a hand-shake sufficient to wrench his shoulder from its socket.

A Live Woman and a
Pretty Doll

A Live Woman and a Pretty Doll

That morning we were told by Joséphine that her master was receiving in the library. So we climbed up to the second floor, that is, to the top of the house, for M. Bergeret has installed his *bibliothèque*, his *"librairie,"* as Montaigne would have said, in the attic of his dwelling. One pushes open an old door, padded with leather, the ancient swinging door of a vestry. On entering one would fancy oneself in a chapel. A mystical light filters through stained-glass windows, ornamented with venerable coats of arms. This gentle light falls lazily upon a low ceiling hung with tooled and gilt leather; it clings to the pyxes, the chalices, the monstrances, the patens, and the censers, with which many cabinets are filled to overflowing.

Anatole France is an enthusiastic collector of religious objects. There is nobody in the world with more ecclesiastical tastes.

In the first place, like a pious anchorite, he dwells on the edge of a forest. It is true, the forest is a pretty little one: the Bois de Boulogne. Fauns

The Opinions of Anatole France

and devils of the female sex are commoner there than wild beasts.

He wears a long dressing gown of clerical cut. It is true, the colour is of a delicate shade and the material soft in texture. He always wears a skull cap like the priests in chapel. It is true, its colour is a revolutionary red. Sometimes he wears a white head dress with pink designs, which resembles an Indian turban. He has adopted this headgear from the region of Bordeaux where he often stays. There the servants wrap their heads in handkerchiefs rolled in this fashion, which give them an Oriental grace.

M. Bergeret, however, much prefers his bonnet of vermilion velvet. It plays an important part in his gestures. Unconsciously he changes its form according to his thoughts. When he is merry, it is provokingly pointed. It is like a caricature of a tiara, or of a Venetian *corno ducale.* At times, when he raises his voice in irony, it assumes the dignity of the *pschent* which was the pride of the Egyptian Pharaohs.

When he is listening to a speaker he throws it back of his neck in order that the passage through his forehead may be freer for ideas. When he is thinking he pulls it almost down onto his nose, as though to withdraw behind a visier.

His profile, with its high forehead and aquiline

A Live Woman and a Pretty Doll

nose, is very long, and its length is increased by the goatee. The lines of his face are delicate rather than vigorous, and give the impression of great and paternal placidity. But the serenity of this mask is belied by the black eyes, terribly dark and prodigiously alive, ferreting and watching on all sides. This glance, sparkling with malice in an almost immobile face, sums up France. It is the sharp edge of his mind which pierces through the beautiful cadence of his melodious phrases.

His whole person is a marvel of harmonious tones. His skin like dulled ivory, his silvery hair, moustache and beard, the red velvet, compose a harmony which would inspire any painter with an irresistible desire to seize his palette and his brushes.

The Master is tall and slender. His natural nonchalance, which increases his charm, gives him the appearance of having a slight stoop. Sylvestre Bonnard, member of the Institute, had "a kind back," according to Princess Trépoff. Anatole France has an affable and ironical back, like Voltaire in Houdon's statue.

To the young writers and the old friends who come to enjoy the flavour of his discourse, he preaches his indulgent philosophy in slow tones and with a slight nasal drawl. And never did a religious orator put more unction into urging belief than France into condemning superstition. His strokes

The Opinions of Anatole France

are all the more deadly because of his indolent manner of speaking. When he seems to be talking to
himself, when he hazards some remark in a most
inoffensive tone, gazing at the toes of his slippers
lined with episcopal purple, it is then that he is
most redoubtable, and suddenly his dark eyes flash
like two sword points.

When talking he likes to stand in the framework
of an immense Renaissance chimneypiece, in which
a man can stand upright. The mantle of this fire-
place is decorated with Italian pictures: saints
gathered about a Virgin who is nursing a *bambino*.
Two little angels in painted wood are also visible,
flitting and playing about.

Let us complete the furniture of the library. In
point of fact, have we not omitted the main thing,
the books?

They cover a multitude of shelves from floor to
ceiling. For the most part they are very old books,
bound in dark brown leather, or well preserved in
a yellowish white pigskin, or encased in the parchment of antiphonaries, embellished with illuminated
initial headings, and with notes of music in red and
black. This last binding was devised by Anatole
France and almost all his friends have copied his
charming invention.

·   ·   ·   ·   ·   ·   ·

A finikin critic was just interviewing the creator

A Live Woman and a Pretty Doll

of Thaïs. He was going to publish in a very serious review a very detailed study of his intellectual development. The Master good humouredly submitted to this curiosity. They ran rapidly over his years at school.

Anatole France was educated at Stanislas College. This calls for no comment, except that something of his religious training remains in his unctuous exterior. After all, it is not a bad education, for it fashioned Voltaire, Renan and M. Bergeret.

Note, said our host slyly, *that I failed at the baccalaureat. This is an important point. Yes, Sir, I got nought in geography. This is how it happened.*

Old Hase was questioning me. This excellent German, a very learned Hellenist, had been appointed professor at the Sorbonne by the Empire, which was internationalist, after a fashion. He was given the task of trying to plough candidates, and he abominated the job.

"My young friend," said he, *with thoroughly Teutonic good nature, "you haf been warmly regommended to me."*

He continued in this strain, but I will spare you his accent.

"Let me see . . . I will ask you some easy questions. The Seine flows into the English Channel, doesn't it."

[133]

The Opinions of Anatole France

"Yes, Sir," I replied with a winning smile.

"Good. Very good. . . And the Loire flows into the Atlantic Ocean, doesn't it?

"Yes, Sir."

"Splendid! . . . The Gironde also flows into the Atlantic, doesn't it?"

"Certainly, Sir."

"Your answers are admirable. The Rhone flows into Lake Michigan, doesn't it?"

Full of confidence, I had not even listened to the insidious question:

"Yes, Sir," said I, still smiling.

"Ha, ha! The Rhone flows into Lake Michigan," muttered old Hase. "My friend, you are an ignoramus! You are an ass! You will get double nought."

We began to laugh. But this anecdote did not meet the requirements of the critic. He sought more serious information.

"I should like some information," said he, "as to your sources. In many of your works, and especially in the *Jardin d'Epicure,* you have given proof of profound scientific knowledge. Could you tell me from what treatises you obtained it?"

"Why, certainly. That is very easy. I consulted a book by Camille Flammarion, which is called I think, "Astronomy for Children." No, I am wrong. The exact title is: "Popular Astronomy."

A Live Woman and a Pretty Doll

The critic nearly fell off his chair.

FRANCE.—*I also get my most solid erudition from Larousse's Dictionary. Yes, Sir, Larousse's Dictionary is a most useful publication.*

The critic could hardly believe his ears.

Our host was assuredly amused at his stupefaction, and purposely provoked it.

My dear Sir, the important thing perhaps is not my scientific attainments, which are slight, but rather the effect of modern discoveries on a mind formed by prolonged commerce with the charming, subtle, humane authors of our country.

He pointed to the old books which burdened the shelves of his library:

There are my sources. You will find there only great or delightful writers who spoke good French, that is, who thought well, for the one is impossible without the other. I have tried to say as well as possible of the things I have seen and learned in my own time what those fine minds of old would have said, if they had seen and learned the same things.

.   .   .   .

Joséphine handed him a visiting card. He put on his huge horn spectacles, for he has an enormous pair, such as one sees in certain portraits by El Greco or Velazquez.

From my friend B——? Show him in.

The Opinions of Anatole France

A very young man, fair, pink and beardless, made his appearance.

What can I do for you? asked France.

THE YOUNG MAN. (rubbing his stomach with a very shiny silk hat)—

"Ba . . . ba . . . bah . . . bah . . . M. France . . . Master . . . you . . . It is . . . I . . .

FRANCE. (very paternally)—*Come, my friend. Won't you sit down?*

THE YOUNG MAN. (crimson)—I have come about . . . I have a little girl cousin who collects autographs . . . so . . . you . . . I . . she . . .

FRANCE.—*She has sent you to get one from me.*

THE YOUNG MAN. (radiant)—Y-yes! Y-yes! Master. I should be happy to do my cousin this favour.

FRANCE. (touched)—*It is an admirable ambition, my child. Where the devil has my pen got to?*

THE YOUNG MAN.—Oh! Master! I do not want to disturb you just now.

FRANCE.—*Then I shall send you what you want. I have your address. . . .*

What does your charming cousin prefer, verse or prose?

THE YOUNG MAN. (in the seventh heaven)— Verse!

FRANCE.—*All right. It is understood. I shall send you some lines of poetry.*

[136]

A Live Woman and a Pretty Doll

Thereupon the youth, covered with blushes, made his bow.

"That autograph is three or four times blessed," said some one, "since it will secure for this amiable youth the favours of his young lady cousin."

FRANCE.—*He flattered me by asking for verse, for I am not a poet.*

There were protests. *Poèmes dorés* and *Les Noces Corinthiennes* were cited.

I have written verse, he said, *yet I am not a poet. I do not think in verse, but in prose, and I turn my prose into verse. Real poets think in verse. That is the distinguishing sign. I knew one who sometimes even spoke in verse, Anthony Deschamps. He was not negligible, and in my opinion deserved more glory. His memory haunts me, because I saw him in striking surroundings. He had been insane. After he was cured he did not wish to leave the asylum, because he had fallen in love with the keeper's wife. We went to hear him recite his poems in the courtyard of the institution. At every verse some lunatic would come and stare into his face, sneer and disappear. Others would crouch down in front of him, stick out their tongues, walk on all fours and dance around us. He gently pushed them away and continued to recite. It reminded one of Tasso among the madmen, or Dante in hell. This fantastic vision still haunts me.*

The Opinions of Anatole France

Victor Hugo also spoke in verse sometimes.

Suddenly our host remarked in the most innocent fashion in the world:

What is poetry, after all? An amusement for children. . . . It is simply the game of corbillon.[1]

"Dans mon corbillon que met-on?"
"Un melon, des oignons, des citrons, des cornichons."

He became serious again.

I should not make fun of it. No. Rhyme is not just a pastime. In our language, where the difference between long and short vowels is so imperceptible, it is the only natural way of strongly marking the cadence. The recurrence of the same sounds divides the phrases into lines of a certain number of syllables, and thus brings out the rhythm more clearly.

Moreover, rhyme is not a difficulty for real poets. As they think in images they command a much larger vocabulary than prose writers, and can easily draw upon it for all their rhymes. What is an image? It is a comparison. Now, all things can be compared with one another: the moon to a cheese, and a broken heart to a cracked pot. So images furnish an almost unlimited supply of words and rhymes. Still better, rhyme calls attention to the image like

[1] *A game in which every word must rhyme with on (Translator's note).*

A Live Woman and a Pretty Doll

the tinkling of a bell. Add the fact that every poet has his own images, his multicoloured epithets, and consequently an immense reserve of rhymes, which is the property of his genius.

Corneille rhymes with heroic words: front, affront, outrage, rage. Racine rhymes with tender and painful adjectives: déplorable, misérable. The rhymes of La Fontaine are mocking; those of Molière are wanton, etc.

The fact is, every great poet discovers his own new world. One finds a land of heroism, another of burning passion; one of mockery and another of generous gaiety. And the imaged rhymes are, as it were, the flowers of those mysterious shores. They grow abundantly beneath the feet of the explorer. He has only to stoop and pick those whose colours harmonize. A bouquet of rhymes is the perfume, the ornament of the shores where each dreamer landed. It expresses the shade of his imagination.

There are, in truth, excellent poets in whose work imagination and feeling take the place of everything else, even of intelligence.

.　　.　　.　　.　　.　　.　　.

"According to Renan," some one remarked, "Victor Hugo's stupidity was stupendous."

FRANCE.—*Yes. No doubt, he was stupid. I agree. But his was the most delicately strung tem-*

The Opinions of Anatole France

perament, and in spite of ourselves we still respond to his thrills. We Parnassians have been accused of having tried to explode his reputation. That is not true. We held him in the greatest respect. We even thought of him as the leader of our little group. That was when we were founding the Parnassian movement. We had foregathered many times at Lemerre's, the publisher's, and the first number of our review was on the eve of publication. We were trying to find something that would draw the attention of the universe to our new-born child.

One of us, I cannot remember whom, suggested that we ask Victor Hugo, then in exile in Guernesey, for a prefatory letter. The idea was received with enthusiasm, and we immediately wrote to the illustrious exile. A few days later an extraordinary epistle reached us:

"Young men, I belong to the past: you are the future. I am but a leaf: you are the forest. I am but a flickering taper: you are the rays of the sun. I am but one of the oxen: you are the wise men of the East. I am but a rivulet: you are the Ocean. I am but a molehill: you are the Alps. I am . . . etc. . . . etc. . . ."

This went on through four large pages, and was signed Victor Hugo.

Together we read this terrifying missive. At the second line we burst out laughing; at the fourth we

A Live Woman and a Pretty Doll

were holding our sides; at the tenth we were in convulsions. Catulle Mendès declared that we were the victims of a hateful trick. This eccentric reply could not have come from the great man. Imperial police spies must have intercepted our request and have tried to play a practical joke on us. But we would not be caught.

We took counsel together as to what we should do. The result of this conference was that we corresponded with Juliette Drouet, who was living at the time in Guernesey, near her deity. We confided our mishap to her and our impatience to have a real letter from Victor Hugo.

Six days later we received a reply from Juliette Drouet. The poor woman was heartbroken. The first letter really was from Victor Hugo. His devoted friend assured us of the fact. She was even surprised at our scepticism, for, after all, she said, his genius was self-evident in these four pages.

Nevertheless, we did not publish the epistle of the sublime poet. Our pious thought was that it would not do him honour. How naïve we were! The gods cannot be dishonoured.

Anatole France continued:

Granted that he was not intelligent. His sensitiveness has influenced that of all his contemporaries. What is most characteristic of the man is those intimate impressions which had never been so

The Opinions of Anatole France

profoundly analysed: the feelings of a lover, of a father at the grave of his daughter, of a mother beside the cradle of her child.

"Sa pauvre mère, hélas! de son sort ignorante,
Avoir mis tant d'amour sur ce frêle roseau,
Et si longtemps veillé son enfance souffrante,
Et passé tant de nuits à l'endormir pleurante.
Toute petite en son berceau!"

That is peculiarly his own. And by insisting upon the store each one of us sets upon the secrets of the heart, he modified our souls. He helped to quicken the life of the emotions.

Oh! I know that many others have reaped the same field, but it was he who bound the sheaves. He was a powerful binder. When one feels with such intensity, intelligence is unnecessary. One has more influence than the cleverest logicians. Even the logicians do nothing more perhaps than express in well-balanced syllogisms the flights of the prophets who are supposed to be lacking in intelligence.

I am very glad, said the critic, to hear you praising the formidable originality of Victor Hugo.

FRANCE.—*He was certainly original ... but, take care! Let us beware of exaggeration.*

All at once, after having celebrated with such spirit the personal qualities of the giant, M. Ber-

[142]

geret, with the habitual pendulum-swing of his un-
bounded dialectical skill, began to point out all that
the author of *La Légende des siècles* owed to tradi-
tion.

*The truth is that what the best poets, the
greatest writers, bring back from their travels in
the realm of fancy is as nothing beside the treasures
accumulated by their predecessors. Victor Hugo is
regarded as a wonderful innovator. But just think.
He owed ninety-nine hundredths of his genius to
others. However original he seems, his versification is traditional. It is the alexandrine. A certain liberty in the caesura and the enjambement, I
admit, but still an alexandrine.*

*Then, his language—did he invent it? Let us
go a step further. The alphabet which he uses. . . .*

ESCHOLIER.[2]—If you talk about language and
alphabet. . . .!

FRANCE.—*What of it? They must, of course,
be discussed.*

*What would our thoughts be without words?
What would words be without the letters which en-
able us to represent them easily. We do not think
enough, my dear friends, about the men of genius
who conceived the idea of representing sounds by*

[2] *Raymond Escholier, who interrupted here to defend the originality of Victor Hugo, has since become the official priest of the
demi-god. He is the Keeper of the museum in the Place des
Vosges.*

[143]

The Opinions of Anatole France

signs. Yet, it was they who rendered possible the dizzy mental gymnastics of the Western world. And those who gradually created speech? Did they not furnish us with the very tissue of our arguments?

Grammatical constructions govern the habits of the mind. So, we can not escape from the influence of those who spoke French before us, who gave it form, and made it famous. Together with their words, their syntax and their rhythms, we have inherited their ideas, which we scarcely enrich. I was wrong in saying that Victor Hugo owed to others ninety-nine hundredths of his genius. I should have said nine hundred and ninety-nine thousandths.

.   .   .   .

Just then Captain X. entered.

He is a Jew, with a hatchet face, a curved nose, hollow, feverish eyes, and a weather-beaten skin, which looked as if it had been smoked: the physique of one who lives on locusts and wild honey. A proselyte to humanitarianism, he is the modern depositary of that flame which so nobly aroused the old crusaders against existing institutions. Like them he is always marching towards the Promised Land, where there is nothing to recall the accursed past.

A Live Woman and a Pretty Doll

After shaking hands with Anatole France, he said:

"You know several of my hobby-horses, amongst others pacifism and negrophilism. I have a new one: Esperanto.

"Yes, I am one of those who are working to establish a common language amongst all men, and to reconcile the workers of the Tower of Babel."

Thereupon, the captain launched into a little propaganda speech:

"Esperanto is the best means of communication for business men. After eight days' practice Esperantists are able to correspond."

FRANCE.—*Gentlemen in commercial life would do well, then, to learn this language.*

THE CAPTAIN.—"But it has loftier ambitions. We have translated a selection of masterpieces from every country. Your *Crainquebille* is one of them, and I have come to ask you to authorize the publication in Esperanto of another of your works."

FRANCE.—*I should not like to rebuff a friend, but I would prefer him not to make such a request of me.*

THE CAPTAIN.—"What is your objection to Esperanto, my dear Master?"

FRANCE.—*Why, nothing. On the contrary, I greatly approve of your zeal in wishing to facilitate*

The Opinions of Anatole France

commercial relations. I should be delighted if it were possible for all men to understand one another without the trouble of prolonged studies. I am sure a universal language would dissipate cruel misunderstandings between them.

But then, is your Esperanto, which would doubtless render great practical services, capable of interpreting even the most fugitive appearance of ideas?

THE CAPTAIN.—*"I assure you that. . . ."*

FRANCE.—*Ah, no! For it is not born of suffering and joy. It has not borne the lamentations and hymns of the human soul. It is a mechanical thing, constructed by a scholar. 'It is not life.*

Come, my dear Captain. Let us suppose that you have been made a present of a wonderful doll. Its big soft eyes are shaded with long eyelashes divinely curved. Its mouth is deliciously red, and is like the pulp of a cherry. Its hair is like spun sunlight. It smiles at you. It talks to you. It calls you "my darling."

Would you love it?

Suppose that you found yourself for a long time alone with it on a desert island, and that suddenly a real woman appeared, even rather ugly, but, after all, a live woman. Is it to the doll you would address your madrigals?

Your Esperanto is the doll. The French language is a live woman. And this woman is so

[146]

A Live Woman and a Pretty Doll

beautiful, so proud, so modest, so daring, so touch-ing, so voluptuous, so chaste, so noble, so familiar, so foolish, so wise, that one loves her with all one's soul, and is never tempted to be unfaithful to her.

We all burst into laughter, and the captain seemed a little peeved. Brousson said to him maliciously:

"Pygmalion breathed life into his statue. Perhaps your passion will effect the same miracle in favour of your doll."

"Young man," said the captain with some heat, "you are sparkling, no doubt, but could you not put a little water in your champagne?"

"And you, Captain," said Brousson, "a little champagne in your water?"

Anatole France interrupted the dispute:

My dear Captain, I will propose a test for you.

THE CAPTAIN.—"As many as you like!"

FRANCE.—*Here are two lines of Racine. I am choosing the most musical, I warn you. They are heavenly music:*

"Ariane, ma soeur, de quelle amour blessée,
   Vous mourûtes aux bords où vous fûtes laissée!"

Come now! Translate that into Esperanto!

Boldly, as if he had drawn his sword to charge at the head of his company, the captain pronounced in a loud voice some words of the idiom which he so ardently extolled.

The Opinions of Anatole France

Come! Come! said France to him very gently, touching his arm. *The verdict is obvious, my dear friend.*[3]

Once again, how could the work of a grammarian, however learned, compete with a living language, in which millions of men have expressed their grief and their joy, in which the laboured breathing of the people and the chattering of pretty magpies in the drawing-rooms are both perceptible; in which are heard the roar of all the handicrafts, the rumble of all revolutions, the death rattle of despair and the murmur of dreams. How beautiful words are, haloed with the memory of long usage!

This word has rung clear as a bell in a line of Corneille. That one has languished in a hemistitch of Racine. Another has gathered the perfume of thyme and wild flowers in a fable of La Fontaine. They all glitter with infinite shades which they have acquired in the course of centuries.

Just think, my dear friend, the words for "laugh" and "cry" have not the same meaning in French as in other languages, because no other man has laughed like Molière, like Regnard, or like Beaumarchais. No woman has wept like certain great Frenchwomen who have loved, Mlle. de Lespinasse,

[3] *M. Anatole France, however, has modified his attitude. Philosophically, he ended by allowing, in addition to "Crainquebille," several of his admirable short stories to be translated into Esperanto.*

A Live Woman and a Pretty Doll

for example. Well, I want my ideas to rest upon words in which the sentiments of all our dead still live.

THE CAPTAIN.—But, then you condemn all translations.

FRANCE.—*Not at all. Have you forgotten the apologue of the doll? The other living languages are real women. And I do not feel any great repugnance to entrust my thoughts to them, however:*

"J'aime mieux ma mie, ô gué! J'aime mieux ma mie."

I prefer my own beloved tongue. I shall be happy, only too happy, if I have been able to add a new beauty to that which I have received so limpid, so luminous, so beneficent and so human.

M. Bergeret Collaborates
with the Divine Sarah

M. Bergeret Collaborates with the Divine Sarah

M. Bergeret does and does not like the theatre. He likes it because a den of mummers arouses his curiosity. He is amused by actors, who have the brains and the vanity of peacocks. He is attracted by actresses, because of their gracefulness, their princely manners, their superb vacuity, or their malicious cleverness, and by the swarm of coxcombs, nincompoops, financial sharks and political puppets, which gravitates about them.

He does not like the theatre because . . . he doesn't.

The art of the stage seems rather clumsy to this subtle logician, who tends a flock of ideas as light and many-hued as the clouds. He has written very little for the theatre. When he composed the *Noces Corinthiennes* he certainly never dreamt that it would one day be performed.

It was produced, however, first at the Odéon, before the war, and afterwards, in 1918, at the Comédie Française. It may be remembered perhaps, that, on the night of the first performance at the

The Opinions of Anatole France

latter theatre, the Gothas dropped on Paris their eggs laden with terror. The harmonious lines were spoken to the heroic accompaniment of the noise of sirens, bombs and cannon. This anachronism, in a classical subject, so far from hurting its success rather increased it. The venerable M. Silvain announced that the performance would continue, and the audience, delighted with their own courage, brought down the house with their applause for both the players and the author who, forgetting his contempt for such solemn vanities, was present at the production.

A farce of Anatole France's is also mentioned, entitled *La Comédie de celui qui épousa une femme muette.* It is a reconstruction of a pretty fable which is mentioned in the third book of *Pantagruel.* He published it in *l'Illustration,* but would not allow it to be played except to an audience of Rabelaisians. However, out of affection for Lucien Guitry he made of *Crainquebille* an exquisite little play, in which the great artist scored a triumph. For the rest, industrious adapters have often displayed the glorious name of Anatole France on the theatrical posters. At the Vaudeville *Le Lys Rouge* thrived for a long time in the glare of the footlights. At the Theatre Antoine, the *Crime de Sylvestre Bonnard* was produced. Gémier was excellent in it, as usual.

It is Gémier, too, who will shortly stage *Les*

[154]

M. Bergeret

Dieux ont soif. Vivid pictures of the French Revolution will whirl amidst the shouting of *Ça ira* and the *Carmagnole*.

Sometimes musicians have attuned their fiddles to the fantasy of M. Bergeret. Massenet religiously offered his crochets and arpeggios to the courtesan *Thaïs.* And lately in the comic opera of the *Reine Pédauque* the good Abbé Jérôme Coignard surprised us by sending forth pleasant trills and skilful quavers, right up to the "flies."

When the libretto of *Thaïs* is mentioned to him, M. Bergeret smiles maliciously:

Gallet confided to me that he would not be able to retain the name of Paphnuce for my hero, because he had difficulty in making it rhyme with noble words. All he could find was "puce" and "prépuce," and he was not satisfied with that. So he chose another name, Athanaël. Athanaël rhymes with "ciel," "autel," "irréel," "miel," which are nice words fit for polite society.

"All right, then. Let it be Athanaël!" I said to him. M. Bergeret added, *mezza voce:*

Between ourselves, I prefer Paphnuce!

One morning at the Villa Saïd a queen of the footlights, Mme. M., was one of the company, and, of course, dramatic art came up for discussion. A young poet mentioned that he was finishing a play.

[155]

The Opinions of Anatole France

FRANCE.—*I congratulate you, my friend, on working for mimes. As they mumble abominably— with a few exceptions, such as our dear M., who speaks verse as divinely as the Muses themselves— as one cannot hear a word they are saying, you are at liberty to display your genius.*

THE YOUNG POET.—"Master, I do not see exactly what advantage I shall derive from their mumbling."

FRANCE.—*What advantage? Ungrateful wretch! . . . Remember that you will not have to be afraid of shocking the public, which will not hear a single word of your text. You will not be compelled to make any concessions. You can say anything. It will be possible for you to express in the most original language the newest and most daring ideas. Is that not the height of bliss for a writer?*

The young poet made a wry face.

France continued:

It must be admitted that in the theatre fine shades are quite lost. Claptrap is the only thing that has any chance of reaching the public ear. Corneille knew that well. His lapidary phrases are models of stage style, but I do not praise him so much for having found those sublime phrases which create an uproar, as for having employed them with a certain discretion. After all, in a pastime of that sort, the most difficult thing is to know when to stop.

M. Bergeret

Que vouliez-vous qu'il fît contre trois?
                    Qu'il mourût!

It is magnificent, and it could go on for ever.
Valère might protest:

Mais c'était votre fils.

Whereupon old Horace would yell in reply:

Mon fils, il ne l'est plus!

Imagine a prolonged jingle of such clashing phrases, and the whole house would become delirious. The method is easy, and we must confess that the great Corneille really used it discreetly.

France continued:

The language of the theatre is not that of literature. Is it worse? I cannot say. For instance, it is often said that Molière writes badly. The truth is, he writes for the ear and not for the eye, that is, in such a way as to overcome the inattention and the weariness of the audience, and the wretched elocution of bad actors. He often repeats the same thing three or four times, to make sure that it is understood. Out of six or eight lines there are sometimes only two that count. The others are simply padding which enables the spectator to rest his mind before coaching the essential words a moment or two later. Listen to Alceste:

Non, non, il n'est point d'âme un peu bien située,
Qui veuille d'une estime ainsi prostituée.

The Opinions of Anatole France

The sense is complete and it is deep enough to arouse reflection. Here is the sequel:

> Et la plus glorieuse a des régals peu chers
> Dès qu'on voit qu'on nous mêle avec tout l'univers.

That is pure nonsense . . . but it is dramatic.

MME. M.—"How hard you are on our poor theatre!"

FRANCE.—*Not at all. Let me explain. It is beyond question that these last two lines are detestable. What is the meaning of "the cheap delights of the most glorious esteem?" What is the meaning of "as soon as one sees oneself confounded with the whole universe?" The repetitions of the same word are horrible. The meaning which one vaguely perceives is exactly the same as that of the preceding two lines. Why, then, this redundancy, one asks?*

It is useful precisely because it is superfluous, that is, because these meaningless words which are not heard give the audience time to dwell upon the two very beautiful lines that precede. Moreover, in that admirable distich, a purist might object to the lameless of the locution "un peu bien." But what of that? That locution is not heard either. The effective words are those which, being placed where the caesura falls, or at the end of the line, are stressed by the rhythm: "âme," "bien située," "estime," "prostituée." These notes ring so clear that

[158]

M. Bergeret

*one is compelled to hear them, and they satisfy the
mind. With the instinct of genius, Molière has always shaped his best lines in this way. The cadence
gives balance to the principal terms, which occur at
the caesura and the rhyme. For example, Dorine
says to Tartuffe:*

> Et je vous verrais *nu,* du haut *jusques en bas,*
>   Que toute votre *peau* ne me *tenterait* pas.

*Observe the spirit infused into the words "nu,"
"jusques en bas," "peau" and "tenterait pas." On
the other hand, Molière often filled up the interstices
with feeble words, simply to preserve the measure.*

*I prefer his prose which is no less substantial, but
does not force him to pad it out. But may be I am
wrong, because in a theatre poetic rhythm, even
when obtained at the cost of a few defects, launches
the words with more vigour.*

Some one wondered that France, in his quotations,
should be able to draw on an infallible memory.

The Master's mocking reply was:

*It is because I was a very bad scholar. All the
lines I have been set to write have engraved many
verses on my memory.*

A moment later:

*There is no denying it, Molière forces us to listen
to him, and he makes us laugh, for it is foolish to
say that he is sad. It was the Romanticists who*

The Opinions of Anatole France

attributed to him their own melancholy. They have made of him a saturnine hero, a Manfred, a Lara, an Obermann. They have denatured him.

He wished to be comic, and he really is. Even his Alceste is gay; yes, indeed, he is gay. He is subtly humorous, only we do not understand him properly nowadays.

My friend Pelletan, the publisher, asked me one day for a preface to the "Misanthrope." I promised it to him. More than once he reminded me of my promise.

"My preface!" he would beg, whenever I visited his shop. Irritated by this, I chanced to reply that I would certainly not write it. He looked so heart-broken that I thought he was contemplating suicide, so I corrected myself.

"I will not write a preface, but a dialogue."

The word dialogue had just caught my eye in the shop window on the cover of a translation of Lucian.

He jumped for joy. His flaming red hair touched the ceiling, and his eyes sparkled:

"A dialogue, excellent! A title page in three colours. The characters in small capitals. The text in italics. A masterpiece, it will be a master-piece!"

What he meant was a masterpiece of typography, for he is convinced that it is typography which makes a writer's talent.

M. Bergeret

*So I imagined the conversation between Alceste
and a critic.*

"You are sad, Alceste," says the critic.

"On the contrary," he replies, "I am a buffoon."

*Then he explains that he is not more than twenty-
three to twenty-five years old. He is in love. He
wants to marry. Now, in the seventeenth century,
the nobles married at twenty-five, at the latest. To
wait beyond that was to depart from good usage.
At forty one was a graybeard. To try, at that age,
to light the hymeneal torch was to invite ridicule.
Arnolphe is forty. It was regarded as unreasonable
of him to have pretensions to marrying Agnès.*

*In Molière an old man of forty is fated to become
a cuckold. It is a matter of course.*

*Alceste, then, is a greenhorn, and the funny thing
is that this young prig, who ought to abandon himself entirely to the carelessness of youth, takes it
upon himself to deliver homilies to everybody. It is
the contrast between his blond wig and his morose
appearance which is the very basis of the comedy.
Note, also that, if he grumbles, it is only when he is
personally offended, when he hears the sonnet which
Oronte intends for Célimène, when he is going to
lose his lawsuit, when rivals make love to his sweet-
heart in his own presence. Misanthropy is merely
a form of selfishness, such is the profound and funny
moral of the play. But modern actors distort the*

*character by making him forty or fifty years old.
Instead of a grumbly young spark, who is comic,
they give us an old bear with a sore head, who does
not make us laugh at all. Thus, an error of detail
renders the whole masterpiece unintelligible, and
gives Molière an air of Heraclitus.*

*It is also customary to paint the cuckoldry of
Molière in the darkest colours, which are reflected
in his works. He is the tragic cuckold. Yet, why
should his cuckoldry be sad, when all the matri-
monial misadventures which he has put on the stage
arouse laughter?*

*At times, it is true, he has expressed sensual de-
sire with an intensity which is almost painful. Do
you remember Tartuffe's declaration of love?
What a mysterious tremor!*

> Et je n'ai pu vous voir, parfaite créature,
> Sans admirer en vous l'auteur de la Nature.

*It is already Baudelairian. But Baudelaire is tor-
tured, whereas Molière mocks the torture of Tartuffe.*

· · · · · · ·

After this little walk round the garden of
Molière we returned to the mummers.

FRANCE.—*They sacrifice everything to their
mania for appearances, and their art, more often
than not, is mere bluff.*

MME. M.—Hm! Hm!

M. Bergeret

FRANCE.—*I beg your pardon, my dear lady. There is no question about you, who are a peerless luminary.*

. . . Provided an actor tops the bill and gets all the limelight on the stage, he cares nothing for the play. And probably he is right, for it is he whom the public come to applaud, not the author. And what self-complacency! Sardou used to play upon just that weakness of his interpreters, the clever rascal! I saw him at work during rehearsals. In order to mortify the stars, and keep them within bounds, he used to pretend sometimes that he could not recall their names. He would say to the most famous actor:

"You, Thingabob, what's this your name is? . . . Anyhow, you who are playing the part of Napoleon . . . you are execrable!"

Then, to a wretched twenty-fifth rate barnstormer, who had a walking-on part:

"Good! Very good, M. Evariste Dupont! I am delighted!"

This apparent praise for a nobody touched the lords of the theatre to the quick, and made them as pliable as wax.

We spoke of the liberties that stars take with their text.

FRANCE.—*Once again, what does it matter, since nobody can hear them. It is sufficient for them to*

[163]

The Opinions of Anatole France

appear to be saying something. Did not some one assure me that an illustrious tragedienne sometimes used to interlard her part with remarks to the scene-shifters. With her golden voice she intones:

Dieux, que ne suis-je assise à l'ombre des forêts!

Then, suddenly, in the same tone of purest gold:

Trois lampes sont éteintes à la deuxième frise.
L'électricien sera mis à l'amende.

Afer that, without any interruption:

Quand pourrai-je, au travers d'une noble poussière,
Suivre d'un œil un char fuyant dans la carrière!

The public does not notice anything and the electrician relights his bulbs.

The anecdote made us snigger.

FRANCE.—*One day, I am told, the supers followed the example of their superior, and began also to talk while on the stage. It was at a performance of "L'Aiglon."*

At a dazzling ball given in the Imperial Palace at Vienna marquises, archdukes and princes had been played by hawkers from the Halles, bedizened with trappings and trimmings, trinkets and gold braid. Unfortunately, as they were somewhat deficient in the usages of court life, the illusion had not been complete. Consequently, during the interval, the queen of tragedy did not fail to admonish them roundly:

[164]

M. Bergeret

"*You marched like a flock of sheep,*" *she shouted,* "*like sheep, like sheep!*"

The next scene is the battle field of Wagram. Our friends the hawkers, who had divested themselves of their fine gala dress, were now representing the dead and dying with which the plain was strewn. They had been told to utter groans whose lugubrious chant was to rise to heaven. Scarcely had the curtain risen than they began to modulate their moans. At first it was a confused murmur, but soon definite sounds emerged:... "arch," "..ik..." "....ock," "... eep".... Then the dying finally droned lamentably a phrase which they pronounced and repeated in perfect unison!

"*We ... marched.... like ... a flock ... of sheep ... a flock ... of sheep.*"

The tragedienne who was listening in the wings was afraid that a phrase so clearly enunciated would cross the footlights:

"*Curtain! Curtain!*" *she ordered peremptorily.*

Thereupon, we spoke of the genius of Mme. Sarah Bernhardt.

FRANCE.—*She was often sublime. Without betraying Racine, she was an entirely different Phèdre. Every generation admires beauties hitherto unknown in the works of great authors. Sarah was our Phèdre.*

[165]

The Opinions of Anatole France

Do you know that I formerly collaborated with her?

Yes, indeed. That is a long time ago. She invited me to come and see her and talk about a scenario she had planned. In the studio where she received me Maurice Bernhardt, still a child, was playing with a huge Dane. The divine tragedienne was talking. Maurice, seeing the eye of the dog glitter, put out his little hand to grasp this shining object. Naturally, the good dog, found this game lacking in charm. It turned away, and unintentionally it sent Maurice rolling on the carpet with a slight movement of its back. Maurice yelled. His mother interrupted her conversation to lift him up and console him. After that, to make sure of being understood, she began her narrative again.

Once more Maurice tried to seize the dog's eyeball. Once more the Dane knocked Maurice down. Again Mme. Sarah Bernhardt wiped away the tears of her offspring and resumed her story. Maurice fell four times, and four times his mother related the beginning of the scenario. A few days later she was to sail for America.

"Good-bye to our lovely collaboration," I said to her.

"Not at all," she replied, "we shall continue our play by correspondence."

M. Bergeret

"By letter?" I inquired.

"By telegram."

"But you are crossing the Ocean."

"The telegrams will be cablegrams, that's all!"

"But," I said again, *"you will be travelling in America. I have been told that it is your intention to go right out to the Far West."*

"You have been correctly informed. That will not prevent us from going on with our collaboration. Across the silent plains of the Far West I will despatch Redskins who, mounting barebacked and untamed horses, will gallop to the nearest town with the text of my cablegrams."

"But . . ." I ventured.

"You are making mountains out of molehills," she cried, laughingly.

I said good-bye to her.

In spite of her desire and mine, our correspondence was not established so easily as she had said Our collaboration ceased. I was very sorry about it. I suspect those damned Redskins of having lost the missives of Mme. Sarah Bernhardt.

"Master, you are charming," said Mme. M., "but your irony will certainly disgust with the theatre this young man who has confided to you his hopes."

FRANCE.—*That is not my intention. In fact, to prove my sympathy, I am going to give him a piece of valuable advice.*

[167]

The Opinions of Anatole France

Young man, if you want to be performed, get a very bad actress for your principal part.

THE YOUNG AUTHOR.—Oh, upon my word! . . .

FRANCE.—*Yes, indeed. The great difficulty for an author is to find a very bad actress of renown. Understand this: To make up for lack of talent she must be very beautiful. If she is very beautiful, heaven will send her magnificent protectors. If she has magnificent protectors, she can perform in every play that strikes her fancy. So, find a very bad actress.*

As he said this, M. Bergeret toyed with a book which he had just received. It was *La Pisanella*, by Gabriele d'Annunzio. The dedication caught his eye and he read it aloud:

"To Anatole France, on whom all the faces of Truth and Error smile equally.

"GABRIELE D'ANNUNZIO."

That is a scratch of his paw, but very neatly done, I must say!

As he has scratched me, here, by way of revenge, is a story I heard yesterday.

At the time when "La Pisanella" was being rehearsed at the Châtelet a reporter came to interview the author, who cheerfully submitted to his questions.

By chance the journalist noticed an old cameo ring on the poet's finger.

[168]

M. Bergeret

"What a wonderful stone!"   he cried.

"Do you like it?" inquired Gabriele d'Annunzio. "It is yours."

Drawing the ring from his finger immediately, he slipped it onto that of the caller, who tried in vain to refuse so generous a present.

Our reporter counted on keeping this rare piece of jewellery as a souvenir of the great writer.   But he was dying to know its value.   He entered the first best lapidary's and showed him the carved stone. The jeweller did not even take the trouble to use his magnifying glass:

"That," he said disdainfully, "is a piece of glass. It is worth about four cents."

Whence I conclude that Gabriele d'Annunzio is an excellent dramatist.

MME. M.—"Very well, Master.   The theatre is the land of deceptive and often clumsy appearances.   Everything in it is a delusion to refined minds.   But is life so different from the theatre?

"My profession brings me into contact with all the bigwigs of the world.   I must tell you of my interviews with them.

"In Berlin, after an evening when I had played before the Kaiser, I was presented to him.   You know that he is an expert in strategy, painting, politics, architecture, diplomacy, music, theology, dancing, dressmaking and cookery. He is also an expert in French literature.

" 'Ach!' said he, 'I love France very much.' (He loves it, no doubt, the way the wolf loves the lamb.) 'Ach! I adore your literature above everything. I adore it! At the present time you are the happy possessors of a great genius. I read his works a great deal. I adore them! I adore them! We have nothing like them in Germany.'

" 'To whom does Your Majesty refer?'

" 'To Georges Ohnet. Ach! Georges Ohnet! Nothing so collossal as the *Maître de Forges* has ever been written.'

"You can see that the Kaiser is an expert in French literature. In brief, this monarch who makes the world tremble by twirling his moustache, is nothing but a perfect imbecile."

Mme. M. continued:

"At the Imperial Theatre at Petersburgh, I was taken to the Tsar's box. It appeared, he wanted to congratulate me.

"Just when I was brought into his presence, it so happened, why I know not, that he was seized with a fit of indigestion. A metal basin was being held in front of him. However, he received me, turned his pale eyes towards me, and Nature, which is no more merciful to potentates than to beggars, caused this wretched puppet to go through a most unappetising

pantomime.   I left without hearing his compliments,
I assure you.

"That is how, at the height of their splendour, the
most powerful sovereigns in the world appeared to
me.[1]   Distance lends enchantment to the view:

De loin, c'est quelque chose et de près ce n'est rien.

"Now, after that, do not tell me that the theatre
is more deceptive than real life."

M. Bergeret smiled and raised the hand of Mme.
M. to his lips.

*I am much obliged for the lesson, my dear lady.
I was wrong to abuse the theatre.   It is much less
mendacious than I pretend, and it certainly resembles
life, since life is so like a stage.*

[1] *At the time when Mme. M. spoke of these two crowned puppets, she took them for characters in a comedy. She little knew
that they would soon act in drama. But, whether comedy or
drama, is it not always the stage?*

Anatole France at Rodin's: Or Lunch at Meudon

Anatole France at Rodin's: Or Lunch at Meudon

Anatole France went one day to call on Auguste Rodin at Meudon. Mme. de N. took him there. She is a Polish noblewoman, of uncertain age, small, smiling, and plump, and lisps volubly a French that is strongly flavoured with a foreign accent. She adores men of genius. She loves them platonically, but passionately. She becomes their slave. She had given her soul both to Rodin and M. Bergeret.

She came to all the gatherings at the Villa Saïd. She used to bring roses to our host and, courtesying, almost kneeling, before him, she would plant greedy little kisses on his aristocratic hands. She did the same for Rodin, when she went to see him in the Rue de l'Université, the Rue de Varenne, or at Meudon.

This idolization of great men is commoner than people imagine, and they have often great difficulty in escaping from it. They are besieged with love-letters. Some women openly make advances to fame, just as men pay homage to beauty.

[175]

The Opinions of Anatole France

France came to the rustic studio of the celebrated sculptor, accompanied by Mme. de. N.

When M. Bergeret goes out he wears a grey felt hat, rather low in the crown. which looks like a cake, because of its broad brim. His overcoat hangs rather loosely on his thin body. Tall, simple, and with a slight stoop, he looks like a respectable taxpayer on his way to his house in the country. He never wears his decoration. As is probably well known, he is an officer of the Legion of Honour. It is a trifle for his reputation, but he himself has been at pains to say, on many occasions, that he cares nothing for official honours. He ceased to wear the rosette at the time of the Dreyfus Affair, by way of protest when Emile Zola was divested of the Order.

Occasionally, amongst friends, he will give a dissertation upon the taste of his compatriots for badges of honour.

Whence this mania? he asks. *Oh, yes. I know. A man with a decoration can wear a soft hat without incurring the humiliating contempt of the concierges. That, at least, is something. He need no longer be so punctilious about his appearance, and the stains on his waistcoat are overlooked. In short, the piece of ribbon is a substitute for benzine. This emblem may also be useful in case of a flagrant outrage on public morals. How could a police spy*

Anatole France at Rodin's

seize in his clutches a gentleman whose buttonhole is adorned with red? But, of course, this supposition is entirely gratuitous, for a man with a decoration is always a man of honour.

I cannot see why French people covet the cross so obstinately. Are they more vain than other mortals? No. I do not think so. Man is the same everywhere, only the manifestations of his vanity differ from nation to nation. The pride of the Italians seizes upon impressive titles: Cavaliere, Commendatore. That of Germans upon parchments: Herr Doktor, Herr Professor. That of the Yankees upon the amount of one's fortune: So-and-So is worth so much, and So-and-So is worth twice that. In short, our appetite for ribbons, braids, medals and stars is perhaps the most harmless and unobjectionable of all.

.   .   .   .

· Rodin was doubtless greatly flattered by the visit of M. Bergeret. Yet, these two prophets did not profess unreserved admiration for one another. In private conversation Anatole France is in the habit of commenting freely upon the inspiration of the celebrated artist.

He is a genius. I am sure of it. I have seen some nudes of his, palpitating with life. But he is not one of those great decorators such as France has known, especially in the seventeenth and eigh-

teenth centuries. He seems to me to know nothing of the science of grouping. Above all, it must be said, he collaborates too much with accidents.

M. Bergeret explains what he means by these rather cryptic words:

He abuses his right to destroy what is not perfect in a work. Dear old President Fallières, who was one day paying an official visit to the Salon, stopped in front of a statue which had neither head, nor arms, nor legs, and said, with great simplicity:

"M. Rodin is certainly a great man, but his furniture removers are singularly careless."

Then M. Bergeret began to draw upon his store of anecdotes:

Do you know how he conceived that Victor Hugo, the half-reclining figure in marble in the gardens of the Palais-Royal? This is the story:

Rodin had just finished in clay an imposing statue of the poet. Victor Hugo was standing upright on the crest of a rock. All sorts of Muses and Ocean deities were circling about him. One morning the sculptor brought a whole troup of journalists to his studio, that they might contemplate the new work. Unfortunately, the evening before, he had left the window open, and, as a terrible storm had broken out during the night, a stream of water had reduced the huge group to formless pulp. The cliff had collapsed upon the dancing deities. As for Victor Hugo, he had flopped down into a sea of mud.

Rodin opened the door, and allowed his guests to go in first. Suddenly he beheld the disaster. He all but tore his beard with despair. But the chorus of praise had already begun:

"Wonderful! — Marvellous! — Formidable! — Victor Hugo rising from this bed of slime, what a symbol!—Master, it is a stroke of genius!— You have tried to represent the ignominy of an epoch in which the inspiration of the bard alone survived, noble and pure. How beautiful!"

"Do you think so?" Rodin asked timidly.

"Of course! It is the masterpiece of master-pieces. Oh! Please, Master, leave it as it is!"

The story is certainly piquant. . . . *Si non è vero.* . . .

In his drawings, continued M. Bergeret, *Rodin represents little more than women showing their . . . And his monotonous audacity is just a little tiring.*

The other day I met him at the house of a friend, and he confided to me with delight that he was doing a series of water-colours with a darling little model.

"This young woman," he said to me, "is absolutely Psyche. . . . By the way, you who are a scholar, could you tell me who Psyche was?"

[179]

The Opinions of Anatole France

As I always try to make people happy, I tried to give him the answer he expected.

"Psyche," said I, "was an obliging young woman, who was always ready to show her. . . ."

"My word!" cried Rodin, "that is exactly the way she appears to me. You have made me very happy."

But I cannot reproach him with his eroticism, added M. Bergeret, *for I know very well that sensuality makes up three-quarters of the genius of great artists.*

I do not pardon him so easily for his too casual habit of appropriating the work of others. I was told lately that a photographer went to Meudon to take photographs of the Master's sculpture. As Rodin was away, he was received by a figure-carver. He noticed a huge block of marble still in the rough, in which only a knee was visible, finely carved. He became most enthusiastic:

"Admirable!" He cried. "Do tell me the name of this masterpiece."

"It is 'La Pensée,'" replied the carver.

The delighted photographer was already focussing his camera, when he was told: "It is not by Rodin, but by his collaborator, Despiau."

The photographer turned to another massive block, from which a nude back emerged.

Anatole France at Rodin's

"Splendid," said he. *"What is the name of that?"*

"Also 'La Pensée,' but that is not by Rodin either. It is by Desbois, his collaborator."

The disappointed photographer perceived a third block, in which a foot stood out.

"Marvellous!" he declared. "What does that represent?"

"Still 'La Pensée.' Besides, that is rather evident! But it is not by Rodin. It is by Bourdelle, his collaborator."

At this, the photographer became desperate, hoisted his camera on his back again, and made off as fast as his legs could carry him.

Rodin, in his turn, sometimes spoke of M. Bergeret in rather harsh terms. Of course, he praised highly the wit of Anatole France and the charm of his style, but he had scanty esteem for the varying shades of his thought, which he considered specious and instable.

He has the gravy, he declared bluntly, *but not the rabbit.*

It should be explained that rabbit was his favourite dish. It was a remembrance of the time when he was a figure-carver and ate his meals in cheap restaurants. Rabbit seemed to him a food of the gods. Obviously, Anatole France lacked something essential when he had no rabbit. Consequently, he would never model the bust of M. Bergeret. He had been commissioned to do so by dear old Dujardin-Beaumetz, the Under-Secretary at the Ministry of Fine Arts, but he never began. Perhaps the extraordinary mobility of such a face discouraged him.

.   .   .   .

Rodin invited M. Bergeret to admire the work which he had on the stocks, and his collection of antiques. Then they went into the dining-room.

Rose, the sculptor's old companion, wanted to slip away. She did not feel at home in the presence of the illustrious visitor. Rodin caught her by the arm.

Rose, sit down there! he said to her imperiously.

"But, Monsieur Rodin. . . ."

I tell you to sit down there!

Rose used to call her companion "Monsieur Rodin" to show her respect for him.

She grumbled again:

"What funny creatures men are! They think you can be in the kitchen and the dining-room at the same time!"

But she sat down with us to eat her soup. During the meal she got up several times, cleared away the dishes, and trotted off into the kitchen to bring in the courses. Then she would sit down quickly.

Anatole France at Rodin's

Rodin would not have any other servant near him.

Rose was a most gentle creature. The life of this woman, timid, discreet, obscured, terrified, in the shadow of that despotic colossus, haloed with glory, would make a story for Balzac. Once upon a time she was a fascinating beauty. Sometimes Rodin would point out in his studio an admirable bust of Bellona, with frowning glance. Then, addressing Rose:

It was you, he would say, *who posed for that Bellona. Do you remember?*

In a tremulous voice she would reply:

"Yes, Monsieur Rodin."

The contrast was striking between this nice little old woman and the terrible helmeted goddess who had formerly been modelled in her likeness. She idolized her great man. She had shared with him the harsh experience of an existence full of ups and downs. He often tortured her, for he was the most fantastic and changeable of men. She used to see lovely women coming into her house, who were her victorious rivals, and she had to bear their presence without a word of complaint.

The slightest attention from him filled her with joy. In her garden at Meudon she passionately cultivated flowers. One day I saw him pluck one and offer it to her:

Here, Rose, this is for you.

[183]

The Opinions of Anatole France

"Oh! Thank you, Monsieur Rodin," she said, swelling with celestial happiness.

Let me complete this sketch of a touching picture with a few more strokes, and recall the last hours of this humble existence.

When Rose's health declined, Rodin married her. And it was as if the gates of heaven had opened to receive her. But her illness was consuming her. She was installed in a wickerwork armchair on the steps, so that the rays of the sun might warm her. Her eyes were too bright in their hollow sockets and her cheekbones a feverish red. She had a ceaseless dry cough.

All of a sudden Rodin realized what he was about to lose. He was well on in years himself. He sat beside her in a similar chair, and looked at her in silence. He put his great hairy paw on the thin, bloodless hand of the poor woman, as if to keep her by main force.

She breathed her last, and very shortly after, the giant followed her to the grave.

· · · · · · ·

The dining-room in which we sat was as spring-like as an idyll. The windows looked out onto the bluish slopes of Meudon, and upon the valley of the Seine, winding lazily beneath a silver sky.

Rose served up a huge dish of rabbit, and Rodin himself fished out rashers and placed them politely

Anatole France at Rodin's

on the plate of Anatole France, whom he wished to honour.

At a certain moment, when the sculptor made a movement to pour some water into his wine, he stretched out his hand towards a square decanter whose glass stopper was curiously ornamented with coloured spirals, like those glass marbles in which urchins delight. Suddenly he said:

Rose, I have already told you that I did not want to see on my table. . . .

Precipitately Rose seized the abhorrent object and fled with it. She returned a moment later with another decanter and said to us:

"M. Rodin would have thrown on the ground the one which annoys him so much!"

We are invaded by ugliness, growled the sculptor. *All the things we use every day are an offence to good taste. Our glasses, our dishes, our chairs, are horrible. They are machine-made, and machines kill the mind. Formerly the slightest domestic utensils were beautiful, because they reflected the intention of the artisan who made them. The human soul ornamented them with its dreams.*

I read in Andersen, the adorable Danish writer, that, when night comes, the furniture and other domestic objects begin to talk amongst themselves. The chandeliers chat with the clock, the fire-dogs gossip with the tongs. As a matter of fact, all the relics of the past speak in this fashion, even during the daytime. They whisper to us a hundred touching confidences about the good people who made them. But our furniture of today is silent. What could it have to say? The wood of an armchair would reveal to us that it was sold in large quantities from a mechanical sawmill in the Northern provinces; the leather, that it comes from a great leather-dressing factory in the South; the copper, that it was cast by thousands in some factory in the East or West. And if they all began to talk together, what a dreadful cacophony. It is sad, you know, to live at a time when the little familiar household deities maintain the silence of the grave.

M. Bergeret admitted that our decorative arts had fallen very low.

RODIN.—*If it were only our decorative arts! But it is art, art pure and simple, which has dwindled to nothing. No distinction can be made between decorative art and art. To make a very beautiful table or model the torso of a woman, is all one. Art always consists in translating dreams into forms. We no longer dream! People have forgotten that every line, if it is to be harmonious, must express human joy and sorrow. And in what is called great art, in sculpture, for example, as well as in the making of ordinary things, machinery has put dream to flight.*

Anatole France at Rodin's

This prophetic outburst disconcerted M. Bergeret a little, for it is not his wont to take such dizzy flights. He brought the conversation down to a more modest level.

How can machinery influence sculpture? he asked.

How? replied Rodin still grumbling. *Why, because casting is a substitute for talent.*[1]

FRANCE.—*Casting?*

RODIN.—*Yes; nowadays this mechanical process is commonly employed by our sculptors. They are satisfied to make casts of living models. The public does not know this yet, but in the profession it is an open secret. Modern statues are nothing more than casts placed on pedestals. The sculptor has nothing more to do. It is the maker of plaster-casts who does all the work.*

FRANCE.—*Allow me to ask a question. I quite understand what you say when the figures of a monument are exactly life size. But what do our artists do when they execute figures larger or smaller than the actual dimensions?*

RODIN.—*There is no difficulty whatever about*

[1] *When Auguste Rodin began he was accused by the academic sculptors of having recourse to the process which he disapproves of so violently. The State, which wanted to purchase his "Age of Bronze," went so far as to appoint a commission to ascertain that this work was not simply cast from living models. It is striking to hear the man of genius, who always spiritualised nature, turning the tables on his opponents, whose uninspired technique assuredly deserves his sharp censure.*

[187]

*that, for they have instruments for enlarging or re-
ducing the casts.*

FRANCE.—*And in ancient times, you say, the
sculptors refrained from making casts of living
models?*

RODIN.—*They used casts only for documentary
purposes. Formerly in the studios one saw arms,
legs, and torsos, in casts, whose contour was perfect. The artists studied them to check the position
of the muscles in their works, but they were careful
never to copy them. They always attempted to put
life into the models to which they referred, to trans-
form them, to breathe into them their inspiration.
It was the Italian, Canova, who began, at the close
of the eighteenth century, to incorporate cast pieces
into his statues. The great number of commissions
which he received forced him to adopt this expedi-
tious method. Since then, his example has been uni-
versally followed.*

*Sculptors have ceased to give their work the
stamp of thought which transfigures objects and
illuminates them with an interior light. They have
sought only vulgar substitutes. Not content with
casting nudes, by a fatal descent they have repro-
duced exactly real clothing. In women's costumes
they have imitated ribbons, laces, trimmings; in
men's clothes, frock-coats, trousers, cuffs, collars, the
whole department of latest fashions. Thus our*

Anatole France at Rodin's

streets and the fronts of our national buildings have become branches of a waxwork museum.

FRANCE.—*It is only too true, my dear Master, and this vulgar realism is also visible in modern sculpture in a quantity of incidentals of ordinary life, furniture which seems to have come from the cabinet-maker's, scientific instruments, objects of all kinds which are a dead weight upon art, for their stiff precision defies imaginative interpretation. A strange collection of bric-à-brac could be made of all the incidental features that disfigure our public monuments.*

The stove of Bernard Palissy would jostle the phial of Pelletier and Caventou, the scales of Lavoisier, the dissecting-table and dead poodle of Claude Bernard, Diderot's armchair, the chair of Camille Desmoulins, Renaudot's press, Doctor Tarnier's hospital bed, the revolving stool of Gérôme, etc. . . . But besides this old curiosity shop, an extensive annex would have to be opened to house the unusually large items such as Chappe's telegraph and the Balloon of the Siege.

RODIN.—*The artists of today do not know that the function of art is to express the human soul, that science cannot be represented by machinery, but by a thinking forehead and brooding eyes; that courage cannot be represented by cannons and dirigibles, but by virile features and resolute breasts.*

The Opinions of Anatole France

Accessories are their supreme resource because they no longer know how to rveal the mind.

. . . .

M. Bergeret, who is very polite, thought it necessary to say that our modern sculpture, nevertheless, was not without a certain distinction. And, as if the allusion were not by himself, Rodin generously cited Dalou, praising his *République triomphante*, drawn by lions in a chariot and followed by Justice and Plenty.

FRANCE.—*Certain critics have disapproved of this mythology, but I do not share their prejudices. Allegory, which is greatly abused, seems to me alone capable of expressing general ideas. Do you not agree with me?*

RODIN.—*Quite right! It is simply a question of rejuvenating old images. Thus, Dalou's Marianne wearing her Phrygian bonnet reproduces the traditional figure of Liberty, but her gesture, so full of friendliness, her face, at once grave and modest, are those of a decent working woman of today.*

FRANCE.—*It is the same in literature. Look at the allegory of Victory. It is extremely ancient and seems exhausted. Yet, read the Proclamation of Napoleon on his return from Elba: "Victory will come charging onward." Is that the Nike of antiquity, I ask you? No; it is his own Victory which*

Anatole France at Rodin's

Napoleon brings thus to the beating of drums.
"Charging onward!" Victory is no longer winged.
She tramps the roads and fields with fury. She is
dusty, dishevelled, plebeian. . . .

Thereupon they agreed that, like every literary
or artistic resource, allegory is effective only by reason of the genius which employs it. The name of
M. Puech happened to be mentioned.

FRANCE.—*Oh! That man terrifies me. It*
sometimes happens that I cannot avoid crossing
the Luxembourg Gardens. They bristle with fun-
ereal monuments to writers, and give me the
unpleasant impression of being a cemetery of
the Muses. But I particularly pity Leconte de
Lisle, in the embraces of a huge winged woman
made of lard. Whenever I see him I fly, thinking
that perhaps one day, beneath those shady trees,
M. Puech will represent the Dreyfus Affair in suet,
kissing my bust, in margarine, on the mouth.

Rodin gave the laugh of a great good-humoured
giant.

.   .   .   .

The two great men naturally drifted into a conversation about the changes which have been made in
Paris. They were both born there, and M. Bergeret, who was brought up in a bookshop facing the
Louvre, on the banks of the lazy Seine, tenderly

[191]

cherishes the memory of the landscape of friendly edifices and trembling leaves, which enchanted his gaze as a child.

They will end, he said, *by making our Paris ugly.*

RODIN.—*As a matter of fact, the old houses which are its noblest ornament are being everywhere destroyed. The politicians, engineers, architects and financiers of today are plotting a damnable conspiracy against the grace which we have inherited from the past. The most brilliant remains of the seventeenth and eighteenth centuries are being demolished by the strokes of innumerable pickaxes. Did they not recently ravage the delightful Ile-Saint-Louis where dream, hounded everywhere, seemed to have taken refuge?*

Virgil has related a dramatic legend. In order to feed the flames of a sacrificial fire Æneas breaks the boughs of a myrtle tree. Suddenly the broken branches begin to bleed and a groan is heard:

"Stop, wretch, you are wounding and tearing me!"

The tree was a man metamorphosed by the will of the gods.

The poet's fable often comes to my mind when I see the vandals laying the ax to the proud dwellings of long ago. Then it seems to me that the walls are bleeding, for they are alive and human like the myrtle tree of Virgil. In the harmonious

Anatole France at Rodin's

rhythm of their buildings do we not hear the voices of the Frenchmen of old? To break a sixteenth century stone mask, a seventeenth century portico, a delicate eighteenth century frieze, is to scar criminally the faces of our ancestors, to strike them on their eloquent lips. What a crime to stifle their voices! If the buildings were even beautiful which are erected in the place of those demolished! But most of them are hideous.

FRANCE.—*They are all too tall. The modest height of the houses was the chief charm of old Paris. They did not hide from view the soft sky of the Ile-de-France. As ground was cheap, they developed laterally. That was the secret of their charm. Ground has become very expensive, and the houses of today grow higher simply because they cannot spread out. That is the reason of their ugliness.*

RODIN.—*They present neither proportion, nor style, nor pleasant details. People have forgotten that architecture, like painting, sculpture, poetry and music, is an expression of the soul. Taste is dying, and taste is the mind of a people expressed in its everyday life; its character made visible in its costumes, its homes, its gardens, its public places. Our society hates the mind. It kills dream.*

He continued:

Are they not now talking of substituting an enor-

The Opinions of Anatole France

mous iron bridge for the light Pont des Arts, in front of the Louvre? It is maddening! There should be only stone in front of the Palace of the Kings. This mass of iron, which threatens us, will cross the river just beside the Pointe du Vert-Galant, it seems.

In this way they will spoil the amazing view composed of the two banks of the river, the Louvre, the Palais Mazarin, the Monnaie, the verdant prow of the Ile-de-la-Cité, and the Pont-Neuf, majestic as a tragedy of Corneille, or a canvas of Poussin. If that view is perfect, it is because from generation to generation Parisians bequeathed to each other the task of embellishing it. Just as the strains of Amphion's lyre raised the obedient stones which formed divine monuments of themselves, so a secret melody has grouped in irreproachable order all these radiant edifices around the Seine, in whose waters their reflection trembles.

Now, all of a sudden, this great masterpiece must be ravaged!

FRANCE.—Practical utility, they say. But, is there anything more useful to a nation than the charm of a city which visibly expresses the mind of the race, sociable, daring, well-balanced, clear and joyous? That is a lesson which, in my opinion, is worth all the iron bridges to the life and the future of a people.

Anatole France at Rodin's

.   .   .   .

After coffee we went out into the garden, and on to the edge of a slope from which the eye could take in the immensity of Paris. As far as the most distant horizon there spread out an ocean of domes, towers and steeples. Through the fleecy clouds the gold and opal rays of the sun shone upon this vast billow of stone. But frequently the smoke from the factories which hummed in the valley spread gigantic black ribbons over this fairyland.

Was it so difficult, asked France, *to remove away from the city these nauseating factories? Is it not absurd to allow the air of Paris to be poisoned continually by the lofty chimneys that surround it? Is it not an odious sacrilege against so lovely a city?*

RODIN.—*Our epoch, in which money rules, tolerates the worst outrages upon the right of all to both health and beauty. It infects and soils everything. It kills Dream! It kills Dream!*

FRANCE.—*But Dreams always rise again, and perhaps it will take vengeance. Perhaps it will soon create another social order less basely utilitarian, and less contemptuous of the spirit.*

Such was the sad discourse held by these two prophets on the hill of Meudon.

On War

On War

M. Bergeret has always detested war. In several of his books, *Le Lys rouge*, *L'Orme du Mail* and *Le Mannequin d'Osier*, for example, he has expressed his hatred with an irony even more powerful than rage. Before the storm broke he would sometimes say that he did not believe in it, because formidable armaments would make it too horrible, and because the governments of Europe, all more or less tinged with democracy, would hesitate before the risks of warfare. At other times, however, like all of us, he was filled with dread.

"It would be madness," he wrote in the preface to *Jeanne d'Arc*, "to pretend that we are assured of a peace which nothing can disturb. The terrible industrial and commercial rivalries which are growing up around us, on the contrary, give us a foreboding of future conflicts, and there is no guarantee that France will not be involved one day in a European or world-wide conflagration."

A tragic prophecy which was to be confirmed only too soon, alas!

During the dreadful years when his native land,

The Opinions of Anatole France

which he cherishes with filial piety, was threatened with destruction, his heart was heavy with grief. Occasionally his conversation revealed the apprehension which he felt at the rise of the spirit of conquest in the allies accordingly as their triumph became more certain.

Immediately after the armistice, when he was taking part in a ceremony in memory of Jean Jaurès, he made in the midst of the excited crowd one of those noble gestures which the latter easily understand and always applaud. Taking the cross of a wounded soldier he pinned it on the bust of the man who had so passionately preached fraternity, and who had given his life for it. In this fashion he testified that the people of France had made a holy sacrifice of their blood to peace, which they would defend henceforth, without flinching, against bellicose madness. Ever since, he has not missed an opportunity of again launching his anathema against war, and praying for a social order from which it will be banished for ever.

．　　．　　．　　．　　．　　．　　．

The following conversation took place at the Villa Saïd some years before the inexpiable calamity. On account of Morocco our relations were strained with our inconvenient neighbours in the East. In the distance the storm was beginning to rumble. This day M. Bergeret began by speaking

of the cross-Channel press, which was taking our'
side against the Germans just a little too blatantly.

England frightens me, he murmured; *she is ex-
cessively warlike. There is no doubt she is brave,
and it may be that she does not fear war for herself. But I have not the slightest doubt that she
fears it still less for France.*

(We laughed.)

FRANCE.—*Oh, the phrase is not mine! At least,
it is merely a variation of the funny threat which a
certain Bermudez de Castro once made against
Baudelaire.*

France was asked to tell the story of Bermudez,
and he did not have to be pressed.

*He was a noble Spaniard. He had been perse-
cuted in his own country for translating "Les
Mystères de Paris." The clericals down there
were so sensitive to offence that our puerile
Eugène Sue seemed devilish to them. So the
translator had exiled himself in France, where he
had been well received by literary society.
Théophile Gautier, Baudelaire, Flaubert, admitted
him to their circle, for his originality amused them.
As an hildalgo he was monstrously proud, and he
was miraculously dirty. In order to know what
he had eaten at his last meal it was only necessary
to look at his great black beard. With all that,
as vain as Narcissus.*

The Opinions of Anatole France

One day when he was dining with his friends he found a deliciously perfumed letter underneath his napkin. It had been put there by Baudelaire. Bermudez sniffed the envelope, fancied he was about to have a pleasant adventure, and shoved the letter furtively into his pocket. Then, as soon as they rose from the table, he went off into a corner by himself to read it. His eyes were flashing, his nostrils quivering, and he sighed with anticipation. Baudelaire and the others were watching him surreptitiously and enjoying every one of his expressions.

This is more or less what the damsel wrote:

"Noble Spaniard, you are so tall and I am so supple; you are dark and I am fair; you are strong and I am beautiful. I love you. Be at the Place Saint-Sulpice tonight at midnight, near the fountain."

At midnight the practical jokers, who had pretended to go home, went off and hid themselves not far from the meeting-place. It was winter, and bitterly cold. The hidalgo was already there, holding himself more stiffly than ever. With his hand on his hip, and his moustaches bristling, he was walking around the fountain. A biting wind swept the deserted square, and lashed the water, which had frozen on the muzzles of the stone lions and formed fantastic white beards.

Bermudez kept walking round and round.

On War

It struck the quarter, then half-past. Phlegmatic and proud, he continued to walk round. Suddenly, from a corner of the square there came a great burst of laughter, followed by the mocking shout:
"Ah, ha! Señor Don Juan!"
Then Bermudez shouted in a fury:
"Ah! I recognize that voice. It is Bodelairre."
He rolled his r's terrifically.
"I will kill him; I will kill him, if I have to die myself. I do not hold my life very dear, but I hold Bodelairre's even more cheaply.
Then he withdrew majestically. Next day he had forgotten his threats.

Charles Saunier, the art critic, took a notebook from his pocket, and wrote down this anecdote.

"I belong," said he, "to the Historical Society of the Sixth Ward, in which the Visconti Fountain is situated. The slightest incidents that take place within this limited area interest us prodigiously. The greatest events that happen in the rest of the world hardly disturb us. But," he continued, "I fancy you have related a similar scene in *Jocaste et le Chat maigre.*"

Ah, yes! said France. *It was precisely the adventure of Bermudez which I attributed to another character.*

The Opinions of Anatole France

An old gentleman who was present cut short this conversation, which he considered frivolous:

"We were talking of a war in the near future," he grumbled. "Well, if it breaks out, so much the better!"

The author of this peremptory declaration was an obscure poet, who has since died. To judge by his remarks, always overflowing with jingoism, his Muse must have been very heroic. But nobody had ever read his poems. He was so swollen with gout that he could not put on his boots. His feet dragged in old shoes laced over huge bandages of white linen. It was in this attire that he went visiting. He coughed, his eyes ran water, and he stammered. He often came to Anatole France's, for he had known him a long time. The Master tolerated him, but he would sometimes say, when he was not there:

Certain old friends would make me doubt friendship, that divine gift. They plume themselves on being deeply attached, and, indeed, they are, like mussels on the keel of a ship. As you know, they are often poisonous!

Nobody had taken up the challenging remark of the gouty bard. But, tapping the arms of his chair with his flabby hands, he continued, between two attacks of asthma:

"We have remained, thank God, a nation of

On War

soldiers! Atchew! We are fond of war! Atchew!
. . . All we ask is an opportunity to fight!
Atchew! We shall go and get back the clocks
which the Boches stole from us in 1870. Atchew!
Atchew!"

France, who had looked at him for a moment
without speaking, said to him gently:

*I admire this fine enthusiasm in a veteran, and I
am sure, if the country is in danger, that the young
men of spirit will pour out their blood generously
for it. But as for the pretence that the French
like war; it is not true. No people ever loved war.
No people ever wanted to fight. At bottom, the
crowd always looks upon fighting without enthusiasm.*

*What particularly distorts the ideas of historians
is the rhetoric of Livy. Now, I do not believe
this Paduan was sincere. He knew very well that
nobody is happy to be exposed to death. But he
said to himself that it was necessary to raise the
morale of the Romans, who were becoming ener-
vated, and he swelled his sonorous periods.*

*The valour which he celebrated is usually at-
tributed to the armies that win victories. We
imagine that they deserved their success because of
their contempt of danger, and that the conquered
armies, on the contrary, were lacking in courage.
These are gratuitous assumptions. Most fre-*

quently it is chance that decides battles. So far as armies are concerned, I suspect them all of being mediocre, and that none will face suffering and death gladly.

Our revolutionary troops have been praised in lyric strains. In this connection I discovered by chance a very edifying little work, by some one called Rozière, "La Revolution à Meulan." I have not the book any longer. I lent it, and it has not been returned: a proof of its interest.

When the country was in danger troops were raised at Meulan as in every other part of France. It was done with great pomp. The mayor assembled the population in the chapel. Drums rolled and the young men swore to conquer or die, they sang the "Chant du Départ," and set off to join the army. . . . But a week later most of them were found in the country around Meulan. When the situation again became critical, the mayor deemed it advisable to make a fresh appeal to the citizens. He reassembled them. The same conscripts were enrolled . . . and returned after a few days' absence. This ceremony was repeated several times with the same actors. Finally, one lone citizen of Meulan remained in the army, one only! They say he became a general. He certainly deserved to.

I fancy it was not very different with the number

On War

of enrolments at the Pont-Neuf, for, after all, when one offers one's devotion to France on the Pont-Neuf, you must understand that it is particularly to show oneself off. To have been seen is sufficient! One's duty has been done.

THE OLD POET. (coughing)—"Come! Come! My dear France. . . . I cannot accept your irony. Military virtue . . . atchew! is fortunately not rare, atchew! and you will grant that . . . atchew! atchew! . . ."

FRANCE.—*Certainly, I will grant you that there are heroes. Even then, they are not always heroic. The true hero admits that he has sometimes lacked courage. I grant that certain troops, in moments of exaltation, brave frightful risks with intrepidity. But from everything we know we must conclude that the majority of soldiers in an army cling desperately to life, and would not expose themselves, if they were not compelled. That is why the little book I have just mentioned, though it obviously does not indicate the state of mind of all Frenchmen during the Revolution, does seem to me worthy of credit. And my own experience corroborates it.*

THE OLD POET.—"Your ex . . . atchew . . . perience?"

FRANCE.—*Yes. . . . Listen. I will give you a very faithful account of some of my impressions as*

[207]

The Opinions of Anatole France

a member of the national guard during the siege of Paris.

The major of our batallion was a stout grocer from our quarter. He was lacking in authority, it must be confessed, because he tried to humour his customers. One day we were ordered to take part in a sortie. We were sent to the banks of the Marne. Our major looked splendid in his bright uniform which had never seen service. He rode a charming little Arab pony which he had managed to get somewhere or other, and of which he was very proud, an all white pony, adorably graceful and frisky. Too frisky, for it proved the poor grocer's undoing. When he was making it prance, it reared up to its full height, fell on its back and killed our major on the spot by breaking his spine. We had few regrets for our leader. We decided to stop, break our ranks and stretch ourselves out on the grass of the river's bank. We lay there all the morning, then all the afternoon. The artillery was thunderng in the distance. . . . We took care to give the cannons a wide berth.

Towards evening we saw some sailors running along the road which dominated the bank of the river. Many of them were black with gunpowder. Wounded men were wearing bloody bandages. These brave fellows had fought well, but they had

On War

to give way to bad luck. *Why, I cannot say, but we began to shout: "Hurrah for the fleet!"*

This shout, which the sailors thought ironical, succeeded in annoying them. Several charged upon us with fixed bayonets. This looked dangerous to us. We rushed headlong from the grassy slopes and put some distance between us and them. As we were well rested and our pursuers were overcome with fatigue, we easily got away from them. We returned to Paris. But our prolonged inactivity weighed upon us and we were very hungry. Consequently, we had no scruples in pillaging a bakery whch we encountered on the way. Fortunately, the owners had had time to escape, so we were not guilty of homicide.

Such was our conduct. I do not boast of it. No; I do not. But I love truth and must do her homage.

THE OLD POET.—"Those are certainly exceptional incidents . . . atchew! I am sure that . . ."

France.—*My dear friend, I should not like to shake your faith. Above all, beware of the notion that I want to belittle my companions in arms. Our enemy was in no wise different from ourselves. Few of them were heroes. Many witnesses saw German soldiers weeping when they were sent into*

[209]

*dangerous zones. And why mock at those tears?
They probably were aroused by the memory of
young wives who would never see their husbands
again, of little children who would never kiss their
fathers.*

But, let me tell you another anecdote.

*Shortly after the war of '70 I happened to be in
X. . . . As I entered an inn I heard great shouts of
laughter, and I saw the natives of the place in a
circle around a robust lad. He was explaining to
them how he had succeeded in avoiding all the
battles.*

*"First of all," he was saying, "I leaves my place
two weeks late. When I sees the sergeant I thinks
to myself he's goin' to blow me up. But I ain't
such a fool; I plays the idiot. To everything he
asks I says: moo, moo, like a cow.*

*" 'What a swine! What a swine!' says he.
'Not a damned thing to be got out of him except,
moo, moo.'*

*"In the end an officer said to me: 'Heh, there,
you idiot! Since you're a farm hand, you know
about horses.'*

"I nods, yes.

*" 'Well, you can take these two nags to Colonel
Bouchard of the Twenty-eighth Regiment, Third
Army Corps. There are your marching orders,*

and food for the three of you, the two beasts and yourself.'

"I nods again, and off we go.

"But, it so happens that I takes the wrong road and the two nags to the colonel of another regiment. This one, as soon as he spots my papers:

"'Hell! what a fool you are!' he says to me, and he puts me on to the right road and gives me a few francs.

"I need hardly tell you that I loses my way again. And all the time the trouble lasted I wanders about from one colonel to another. But once peace come, I takes my two nags straight to the right colonel of the right regiment. And here I am."

Now, the cynical confessions of this rascal were greeted with sympathetic laughter.

I do not assert that the same audience would not have responded to a narrative of great devotion to duty. The roughest men, if they admire cunning, also venerate nobility.

However, the gallery did not blame this slyboots. The crowd has always a fund of indulgence for Panurge when that unpleasant accident befalls him in the fight, for Sosie, when he gorges himself with ham and wine in a tent far from the battle. It really seems to me quite impossible that the plain *people can ever be infected with the jingoism which infects our middle-classes from time to time. On the contrary, I notice that anti-militarism is bolder than ever. Formerly the deserters, and the slackers, never tried to defend their conduct.* "We are betrayed," *they would shout.* "We are sold!" *That was their only justification.*

Now they have a theory and reasoned motives. "Le Chant du Départ" *has been replaced by a hymn* "Pour ne pas Partir." *To set one's refusal to march to music, is to become glorious.*

THE OLD POET.—"So you approve of them?"

FRANCE.—*Do not put into my mouth what is not in my mind. No; I do not approve of them, for in the present European situation they run the risk of helping the worst enemies of civilization.*

THE OLD POET.—"So you admit that one's country. . . "

FRANCE.—*I admit that our country would deserve to be passionately defended, if it were threatened. And then, we must clearly see in what way it has a right to our affection. If by the word country is meant the sum of great ideas and profound feelings which differ from one country to another, and constitute French wit, English good sense, German dialectics, that is certainly a treasure which should be dear to every nation. It is a flag of light planted on each territory. The finest geniuses of each race have borne it higher and higher. After the event, and gradually, they have given a magnificent spiritual significance to these groups which the fortuitous circumstances of history had originally brought together haphazardly.*

But these moving national doctrines, if they differ, are not divergent, at least. The most eminent thinkers clasp hands across frontiers. They have neither the same tendencies nor the same thoughts, yet they are brought together by their humanity, by their compassion for their fellow-men. It is, therefore, by a culpable deception that people try to oppose one national consciousness against another. On the contrary, in their most serene expression they are complementary. A man can adore his own country while revering others.

Unfortunately, a country is not only a collection of radiant ideas. It is also the business address of a host of financial enterprises of which many have little to recommend them. More than anything else it is the antagonism of capitalistic appetites, often most illegitimate, which drives the nations into conflict, and causes modern wars. Nothing could be sadder. From the bottom of my soul I wish my country to abstain from all greed which might make her in the slightest degree responsible for a struggle. But if she were ever invaded by a covetous neighbour, it would be the duty

The Opinions of Anatole France

of her sons to fly to her help. It would, indeed, be the darkest calamity if France were diminished, for after all, do you not agree, our country stands for very generous aspirations?

THE OLD POET.—"Ah, ha! you see . . . at-chew! Chauvinism has its good points."

FRANCE. (emphatically)—*Not at all! It is criminal folly. When the jingos say that war is sublime, that it is the school of all the virtues, that it refashions and regenerates men, that Providence gives victory to the most worthy, and that the greatness of a people is measured by its victories, that is, by massacres in which its own children perish with the enemy, they are ridiculous and odious.*

THE OLD POET.—"But how will you per-suade people to sacrifice themselves to their country?"

FRANCE.—*By making the country always better, always more just, more maternal towards the people . . . more loyal, more fraternal towards other nations . . . by ceaselessly repeating that war is abominable, by carefully avoiding all the tortuous intrigues which might provoke it . . . by proving by the striking frankness of our conduct that we do not wish to take up arms, that we shall use them only to defend our liberty.*

Then the people will love their country which

On War

*will be identified in their hearts with the finest fu-
ture of the human race.   And if, by any misfor-
tune, it is attacked, they will not allow it to suc-
cumb.*[1]

[1] *Such were the opinions of M. France at that time.   By ad-
hering to communism he has since testified that only the inter-
national organization of the proletariat seems to him capable of
preventing the return of war.*

The Russian Revolution
at the Villa Saïd

The Russian Revolution at the Villa Saïd

It was during the cold season. When Joséphine opened the door for me I saw the hall littered with overcoats, mufflers and furs. The clothes of M. Bergeret's friends were piled up on chairs and consoles. Hats were hanging on lovely rococo chandeliers. Overcoats were thrown over the bottom of the gothic bannisters of old carved oak.

"Are there many visitors?" I asked Joséphine.

"Too many," she replied in a surly tone. "There are heaps of Russians."

Joséphine had little sympathy for the Slavic race.

"It is hard to know,"' she went on, "why the Master receives such people. They're full of fleas. Just look at those old topcoats."

As she spoke she felt with her thumb and forefinger a wretched Inverness, all threadbare. She continued to mutter between her teeth.

"These Russians, they're good for nothing except making dirt about the house. And I'm sure they have bombs. If the Master would listen to me, he would choose his society more carefully. Celebrated as he is, he ought only to see the best people."

The Opinions of Anatole France

I left her to her bad humour.

In the library I found several Russian revolutionaries with the Master. Amongst others there was K. the famous sociologist, a colossus with long fair curly hair, stray hairs all over his face, large blue eyes, surprised and tender, and a smiling, infantine and beatific expression—the perfect type of the scholarly anarchist who candily overturns society with his ideas.

It was the time when Nicholas II was beginning to struggle against the revolt of his people, grown tired of the knout and the nagaïka. S. the Petersburgh newspaper correspondent, who had undertaken a tour of lectures against Tsarism all over France, was giving an account of a speech he had made the previous evening at Valenciennes.

"A most sympathetic audience," he said, "which seemed well informed on the subject."

FRANCE.—*In other words, nowadays the provinces are on the same intellectual level as Paris.*

S.—"Except certain regions; for example, Brittany."

FRANCE.—*It is true, the Bretons are backward. That is partly due to their ignorance of our language. If they understood it, they would perhaps be more favourable than others to certain of our social ideas. Thus, I believe they would readily accept collectivism. They have been prepared for*

*it by the habit of common ownership, which is fre-
quent with them as in all poor countries, for at present it is only the worst land and the poorest pas-
ture which can remain common property, while the
slightest fertile bit is at once seized upon. Unfortunately, we have no speakers who know their
dialect.*

Their drunkenness is also fatal.

*At all events, during my last stay at Quiberon
they seemed to me to be very backward. They
apply none of the new methods of fishing. It is in
the most haphazard fashion that they go out for
fish. They never think of telegraphing to each
other the movements of the shoals. When it comes
to selling they do it under the most heart-breaking
conditions.*

*The fishwife who sells the haul is a big, substan-
tial beldame, who waits for them on the shore and
anxiously watches for their return. As soon as
they land she takes them all to the public-house,
where she makes them drunk, and it is when they are
drunk that she settles with them for the purchase
of the haul.*

*Observe that she is an intermediary with whom
they could quite well dispense. Often the merchant
who is going to send the fish to Paris is also waiting, right beside her on the shore. But it never
occurs to them to deal directly with him.*

The Opinions of Anatole France

What has confirmed me in my unfavourable opinion of their intelligence is a conversation which I overheard between two Breton women. I assure you I was not eavesdropping, for they were separated by half a kilometre, and it was at this distance that they apostrophized each other at top of their voices, like heroes of Homer.

One of them shouted—note this carefully, said France to the old sociologist—*she shouted: "You are a dirty dog, to go with my man!" And the other replied, in the same tone: "If your man goes with me, it is because I am a better made woman than you are."*

Now, I do not know, Sir, if you agree with me, but that retort seemed to me to denote the most complete absence of psychological observation. It is certain that, if we love one woman more than another, it is not because her physical charms seem greater, but for a host of very different and very complex reasons.

The venerable sociologist endeavoured to form an opinion, but without success. A moment later France said to him:

Father Gapon must be pleased: the Russian revolution has come to a full stop.

Then addressing the other persons present:

Our friend S. introduced me to this priest of which we hear so much. He brought him here to the house. He is a robust young man, with dark hair and tanned skin. I timidly confess that he did not make a very good impression on me. He is verbose and emphatic. As he does not know a word of French, S. translated what he said and took it upon himself to curtail it. Gapon noticed this and flew into a great rage.

"He is scolding me," said S., "because I cut short his last sentence, in which he compared Nicholas II to a tiger. What he said was: "He is a tiger thirsty for human blood.""

Well, that quarrel about a metaphor seemed to me in bad taste. After all, every royal or imperial tiger thirsts for human blood.[1]

Gapon, who led the first processions of the strikers at Petersburg, believes that the people must be granted some respite before asking new efforts of them. I do not know if he is right, but the danger is that the halt may become a long de-

---

[1] *It may perhaps be recalled that this Gapon was an agent provocateur, in the pay of the Tsarist police. In Petersburgh he placed himself at the head of a great working-class demonstration, and disappeared just at the moment when the machine-guns were mowing down the crowd. Shortly afterwards he came to France, and it was then that he called at the Villa Saïd. Then he went off to the Côte d'Azur to have a good time with the price of his treason. He met with the end he deserved. Having secured proof of his infamy, the Revolutionaries lured him into a trap and executed him. When he visited Anatole France, he was still unsuspected. Yet, as the dialogue noted here shows, M. Bergeret was not his dupe.*

The Opinions of Anatole France

lay. Maybe the Russians are still too much en-slaved and too unhappy to desire liberty passion-ately. It is a fact that almost all revolutions that succeed permanently limit themselves to confirm-ing results already achieved. Look at that of '89. It was the centres already freed from feudalism which arose and demanded the abolition of the old order. As for the provinces, which were still galled by the traditional yoke, they had so little thought of shaking it off, that they shed their blood oppos-ing the revolution. That was the case of Vendée and Brittany.

Similarly with socialism. It numbers its staunch-est adherents in the big unions, like the miners, who, thanks to their discipline, are precisely those who have already obtained a good part of the ad-vantages promised by socialism. Whereas the most obstinate opponents of this doctrine are the peasants, who suffer most from the bourgeois system. The fact is, social changes take place only when they are ripe. That is why I wonder whether the Russians are not still too greatly deprived of the benefits which revolution would procure them to be willing to fight for them.

K. protested that his compatriots were more en-lightened than people imagined.

FRANCE.—*And is their devotion to the Tsar not an obstacle in the way of their emancipation?*

[224]

Russian Revolution at Villa Saïd

K.—"The religious respect of Russia for its sovereign has quickly evaporated. Our people are mystical, but perspicacious. Having proved the Tsar's lack of good faith, they have turned away from him. Their piety remains intact, but they jump an intermediate stage and address themselves directly to God."

"They are more intelligent than the Breton fishermen," some one remarked, "they suppress the middleman."

K.—"Moreover, it is wrong to picture the Russians as blindly submissive to their priests. On the contrary, though pious, they do not care much for the clergy. When they kiss the hand of a pope they mean to do homage, not to the cleric, but to the God he represents."

FRANCE.—*You do not surprise me at all. Contempt for priests is quite compatible with piety. Usually, the populace detests the cassock. Why? No doubt for the simple reason that is is lugubrious and evokes the idea of the extreme unction.*

But, tell me, is not Russian mysticism contemplative, by preference, and opposed to action? For instance, does your prophet, Tolstoy, not preach resignation to the moujiks, and what he calls "non-resistance to evil?"

K.—"Between ourselves, nobody listens to him. Our workmen and peasants are rough fellows, and it is not easy to put them to sleep again, once they have been roused."

FRANCE.—*Yes, I understand. Moujiks become wolves more easily than wolves become sheep. Indeed, that is truth which your compatriot, Prince Troubetzkoy, recently tested in Paris, where he lives. Just as Tolstoy invites men to bleat, this prince had undertaken to tame wolves. He had caught two of them very young. He had reared them and led them on a leash like dogs. In order to wean them from their instincts he fed them chiefly on vegetables, and the strangest thing is that, for some time, they appeared to be satisfied with this diet. But the other day one of them suddenly planted its claws in the arm of the fruiterer from whom the prince himself condescended to buy the meals of his pets, and they had great difficulty in making this wicked wolf let go.*

There is no moral, by the way, to this story.

K. (laughing)—"Nevertheless, there are sociological conclusions to be drawn."

FRANCE.—*If you like . . .*

K.—"It seems to me the best way to help the progress of liberalism in our country at this moment is to advise other nations, and especially the French, not to subscribe to the Russian loan until the Tsarist government has put a liberal constitution into force."

Russian Revolution at Villa Saïd

FRANCE.—*I hope with all my heart that these tactics will proceed, for it would save thousands of human lives. Unfortunately, it is certain that, if the Russian government found itself supported by our money, it would not hesitate to plunge into the most atrocious reaction.*

K.—"It is preparing for that."

FRANCE.—*It is even possible that it may succeed in stifling for a long time all desire for independence.*

K.—"No; for reaction would soon call forth Terrorist reprisals. But it is important to facilitate the task of the Liberals, and, as you say, to save human lives."

FRANCE.—*Alas! Every human advance consumes too many.*

C'est un ordre des dieux, qui jamais ne se rompt
De nous vendre bien cher les bienfaits qu'ils nous font.
    L'exil des Tarquins même ensanglanta nos terres.
Et nos premiers consuls nous ont coûté des guerres!

A young Slav, very dark, with long hair plastered with bear's grease, a Mongol complexion, high cheek bones and the drooping moustaches of a Kalmuck, suddenly broke the silence which he had hitherto preserved. He spoke French with extreme difficulty:

[227]

The Opinions of Anatole France

"For the success of the Revolution it would be better to. . . .

FRANCE.—*Do you not admire the power of our great Corneille?*

THE YOUNG SLAV.—"Yes; he is wonderful . . . would be better to. . . ."

FRANCE.—

L'exil des Tarquins même ensanglanta nos terres
Et nos premiers consuls nous ont coûté des guerres!

That is more than poetry; it is more than eloquence . . .

THE YOUNG SLAV.—"The Revolution. . . ."

France.—*It is monumental!* . . .

THE YOUNG SLAV. (obstinately)—"Yes, yes. . . . You are mistaken in hoping that Tsarism will abdicate. . . . No confidence. . . . It would be better to suffer atrocious persecution. It would be better to have many martyrs, a great deal of bloodshed, and then the government swept away by an infuriated people."

FRANCE. (addressing his guests)—*This young man, as you see, is a pure-blooded revolutionary. If necessary, he would throw bombs!* . . .

The dynamiter began to smile. From his coat pockets he drew two steel tubes. Then, in great triumph:

Russian Revolution at Villa Saïd

"Bomb in two parts. Separated; nothing to fear. If the two halves are screwed together, the whole house blow up."

FRANCE. (politely)—*Do not screw them, please. And take my word for it, my young friend, as long as there are other means, we must have recourse to them.. Remember this: homicidal justice, even when administered by a people struggling for freedom, can never be anything but a wretched substitute. It is not good to quench with blood the thirst of the gods.*

.   .   .   .

He resumed:
The cause of the Russian revolutionaries concerns us much more closely than people imagine. If they were defeated the spirit of liberty would undergo a crisis all over Europe. On the other hand, their victory would give a great impetus to socialism in other countries, and especially in our own.

The conversation turned to the French revolutionary party.

FRANCE.—*The people in our country are, I believe, very favorable to collectivism. But they have only an instinct where their interests are concerned, and remain shockingly indifferent to ideas. Recently at Bordeaux I had occasion to question two coopers who had been present the previous*

The Opinions of Anatole France

evening at a lecture by Jules Guesde. "Did he speak well?" "Certainly!" "Did you understand everything he said?" "Of course!" It was quite obvious. "He wishes coopers to be happy!" That is all they remembered.

Another anecdote. A few days ago I was at the Bourse du Travail, in the office of the redoubtable Pataud, the secretary of the Electricians' Union. You know whom I mean. Pataud, who has merely to move his finger to plunge Paris into darkness. On the floor around him there were piles of pamphlets. Good! I said. You are trying to educate your comrades, for these, I suppose, are doctrinal works intended for them.

"Those," he replied, "are copies of 'Sherlock Holmes.' The members of the Union cannot stand any other kind of literature."

Then France concluded:

If our party were better organized, if it were not divided into thirty-six fragments, it could organize more persistent and more methodical propaganda, and our principles would have a more thoughtful reception from the working classes.[2]

.   .   .   .

[2] *Anatole France has not lost his interest in the Russian revolutionaries.*

One day Gustave Hervé brought him a young man of thirty-five years, pale, with the close-cropped hair of a convict, and an enigmatical sneer perpetually on his emaciated face.

Russian Revolution at Villa Saïd

(turning to a young engraver) *Just look at these plates by Hans Burgmair, and tell me what you think of them! This lord and his lady embracing: how touching they are. Look at the lady's big belly. It is not because she is pregnant. At that time fashion demanded that the women should have*

The editor of the "Guerre Sociale" introduced him:
"Boris Savinkov, assassin."
"Delighted," said M. Bergeret, holding out his hand to the stranger.
"I must ask my friend Hervé to have a hundred visiting cards printed for me with the title he has given me," said Savinkov jokingly.
"Whom has he assassinated?" asked France.
"The minister Plevhe and the Grand Duke Sergius," replied Hervé.
"Big game," declared M. Bergeret.
Afterwards Savinkov became a minister under the Kerensky government. He vainly tried to resist Bolshevism. He had to leave Russia. From the other side of Europe he tries unceasingly to raise up adversaries against Lenin and Trotsky. This erstwhile Terrorist is now labelled a reactionary. This is not the least paradoxical turn of his fate.
Another Russian, M. Rappoport, who has become a French citizen, and who has a deep and unshakable sympathy for the Bolshevists, keeps up a warm friendship with Anatole France. The truculent portrait of him by the painter Van Dongen is well known. A tobacco jar furnished with a red beard which hides the features almost completely. In the midst of this beard two gold-rimmed glasses glitter. He is a Diogenes or a Menippus thrown into modern society. He speaks with a strong accent, and launches a continuous stream of amusing and cruel witticisms which hit at socialists and bourgeois indiscriminately. During the war he went many times to Touraine, to La Béchellerie where France had retired. He used to turn his host's library upside down, stuff his

The Opinions of Anatole France

big bellies, just as today it commands them to have none. What bold lines! What a lovely harmony of composition!

After all, from time to time one must enjoy what is the greatest consolation in life.

pockets with venerable tomes of the sixteenth century, and enjoy them lying flat on his stomach under the willows in the meadow. After his departure M. Bergeret would ask his secretary to pick up among the tall grass the volumes which failed to answer the roll-call. One day a precious Ronsard was found astride of the wire clothes-line.

During a bombardment of Paris by Gothas an unpleasant adventure befell M. Rappoport. Denounced because of alarmist statements which he was alleged to have made in a cellar, and which some over-zealous patriots pretended to have heard, he was locked up. Anatole France did not hesitate to write him a letter which was read in court and saved the prisoner. In it M. Bergeret said that M. Rappoport's ideas were well known to him, that they were sound, and that the imprisonment of such a man was a scandal. It is certainly M. Rappoport's influence of late which has inclined Anatole France more and more to communism.

The Omnipotence of Dream

The Omnipotence of Dream

There was a vacancy for one of the Paris seats in the Chamber of Deputies. A delegation from the Socialist Party came to propose that M. Bergeret should stand for election. That showed how little they knew him. He is nothing of a politician. He often speaks in public, but very much against his natural inclination. "Comrade Anatole," as he is sometimes called at these meetings, is not an adept in the art of oratory. By striking contrast, he is a divine talker. He is a magician of words. Now tender, now mocking, he speaks like a book, like the most exquisite of books.

At a public meeting he has difficulty in finding words. He reads his speeches. He intones them in a nasal voice which is not lacking in solemnity. If he has to improvize, he stammers, and loses his head. This emotion itself is the most delicate compliment to the crowd which, proud of intimidating a man of genius, applauds him frantically. But in Parliament his opponents would not perhaps be so well disposed. Another insuperable defect! He never replies to letters. He does not even

The Opinions of Anatole France

open them. Formerly they used to pile up on a
tray until old Joséphine burned them. It was a
ritual of this faithful servant. Also note that M.
Bergeret forgets appointments, or else he presents
himself a day too soon or a day too late. The
voters would soon tire of such a representative.
As a matter of fact; the tricoloured sash would
suit this philosopher about as well as a hat would
a monkey.

Consequently, on this occasion he declined the
perilous honour extended to him. The delegates
insisted. He stuck to his refusal.

*I am flattered and touched by your proposal, but
I have not in me the stuff of a representative of the
people. But, at least, do not accuse me of des-
pising politics. On the contrary, I admire the in-
trepid spirits who consecrate their lives to it, and
who, of course, stand for sound ideas, that is, ours.*

Thereupon the name of Jean Jaurès came to
his lips. Anatole France professed the deepest
friendship for him. He liked him for the agility of
his mind, for the prodigious range of his knowledge,
and, above all, for the greatness of his character.

What a noble conscience! said he. *Sometimes
he is unskilful by dint of honesty. He is not afraid
to challenge the passions of the mob. He even
irritates his own partisans by his opposition to their
extremism, and by his loyalty towards his adver-*

[236]

The Omnipotence of Dream

saries. He has elected the most ungrateful part. He tries to be the mediator between the workers and the bourgeois, and to avoid violence...It is a fine task, but a hard one.

Sometimes in a strike, when the military call upon the workers, who are brandishing paving-stones, to disperse, an heroic man, to prevent blood-shed, will advance into the danger zone which separates the opposing forces. Amidst the rumbling of the storm, he preaches calm, thus running the risk of receiving both the bullets of Law and Order and the stones of the rioters. That picture exactly represents the mission which my friend Jaurès has assumed and the threats which he must face.

We remembered those words later on, when the celebrated orator tragically perished, and they seemed prophetic.

A moment afterwards France praised the disinterestedness of Jules Guesde.

What strength this man finds in his poverty! He always wears the most modest clothes; but even his demeanour suggests poverty, and would do so, even though his clothes were less faded. It must be admitted, his rôle is not so arduous as that of Jaurès. It is less difficult to refuse obstinately to collaborate with the middle class than to try to reform it. The hostility which exists between these two leaders of socialism frightens the pessimists.

The Opinions of Anatole France

And the profound divisions in our party are often interpreted as signs of weakness. But they are rather signs of vitality, I think.

There was some astonishment.

Yes, indeed! he resumed. *Just think. There will never be such lively dissensions amongst the leading revolutionaries of today as there were among the early Christians, between Saint Peter and Saint Paul, for instance. In the first century there were assuredly Pagans who were nearer to Paul than Peter was, the Syrians, amongst others. Yet, so far as I know, Christianity has not proved abortive. In fact, it has not succeeded too badly. And it is on the same day, it is together, that Peter and Paul are celebrated. So everything leads me to believe that the socialists of the future will celebrate Jean Jaurès and Jules Guesde on the same date.*

We laughed.

Then M. Bergeret spoke of Briand, who was for many years his friend.

For many a year he planned to leave us in the lurch. He used to get impatient with the ambitious young men who tried to overthrow him at congresses.

"I have let them walk on me long enough," he would grumble.

Do you not think that a nice metaphor? It well

The Omnipotence of Dream

describes that tactics of those newcomers who, in order to gain the confidence of meetings, begin by trampling on the speakers of renown.

Briand accepted very reluctantly the desision of the congresses against socialist participation in bourgeois government.

"It is a great pity," he said to me, "a great pity! There are four or five of us who would do very well in the Cabinet."

I am sure that, amongst those four or five, he counted himself as equalling five or six. He has attained the power he so ardently desired, and he wields it with skill, for he understands the art of governing men.

I remember that, at the time when he used to speak at popular meetings, he was wonderfully clever at working up the public. One day at a meeting he was near me on the platform. The audience was cold, and the most inflammatory rhetoric could not make it thaw.

"Wait," Briand whispered to me, "I am going to 'enliven' the discussion."

In the middle of the crowd he noticed an honest booby who, with eyes and mouth wide open, was not saying a word.

"Comrade!" he shouted, "why do you keep interrupting?"

"I?" replied the other, utterly flabbergasted.

The Opinions of Anatole France

"*Yes; you! You ought to know that a loyal opponent attacks openly. Come up on the platform.*"

"*Speech! Speech!*" *yelled the crowd.*

They jostled the poor fellow, who was trying to get away. Suddenly he was grabbed by half a dozen madmen, who hoisted him up onto the platform. He got there head first. For half a second I beheld two legs struggling desperately in space.

"*Throw him out! Throw him out!*" *shouted the mob. And the two legs disappeared in the confusion. The ice was broken, and the audience, its appetite whetted by this summary execution, listened to the speakers with edifying sympathy.*

M. Bergeret continued:

Recently again, Briand gave proof of his great enterprising spirit. It was the day when old Cardinal Richard was leaving the house of 'M. Denys Cochin, whose guest he had been, to take possession of his new house in the Rue Barbet-de-Jouy. Briand, who was then in power, was afraid that there might be hostile demonstrations against the Archbishop on his way. So he devised this scheme.

He sent policemen in plain clothes in front of M. Denys Cochin's house. When the prelate's carriage came out, the police shouted at the top of their voices: "*Long live the Archbishop! Long live the Archbishop!*" *Unyoking the horses they got be-*

The Omnipotence of Dream

tween the shafts, as if to show their fanatical devotion to the Cardinal. Then they pulled the carriage, pushing and shoving and shouting hurrahs, and made off at top speed. When they met fervent young Catholics who cheered the venerable old gentleman, they jostled them, and continued their way as fast as their legs could carry them. They covered the distance in no time, rushed the Archbishop into the house and closed the door on him. And in this fashion the trouble was avoided which the goverment feared. It is by such subtle artifices that political wisdom may be recognized.

I praise that quality in others, and it seems almost miraculous to me, for I feel that I am quite destitute of it. That is why I should make a very poor deputy. Yes, yes! I assure you. Moreover, I prefer my trade as a philosopher. My foolish vanity leads me to think that it also has its uses.

Then M. Bergeret developed the parallel for which we were waiting.

I know very well that the dreamer is a person of little consequence beside the politician. The politician is the idol of the mob. He is its master and its slave. He drags in his wake the whole tribe of those who seek favours. He is influential, celebrated, famous. He holds in his hands the destiny of the people. He leads them to prosperity or to ruin. He makes the laws, and that, more than

The Opinions of Anatole France

*anything else, seems to denote his power. To make
laws, to draw up regulations which the crowd must
obey, to set the limits beyond which no citizen has
the right to go, is that not almost divine sover-
eignty?*

*There is only one reservation to be made, that
is, laws never regulate anything. When the author-
ities formulate a law it has long since passed into
common usage. It can merely sanction custom.
If it does not, it remains a dead letter. Above the
legislator there are accepted customs. Now, by
whom are these established? By everybody, but
particularly by the dreamers. Is their mission not
to think for the community? In order to think,
training is necessary, as it is for manual labour, for
commerce, for seamanship, for house-building.
I do not know whether the men who cut and polish
ideas have more merit than other mortals. At
least, when they play their part well, they are entitled to some gratitude.*

*In many ways they make life better for every-
body. In his laboratory, from his quiet courtyard,
the frail, bespectacled man of science reshapes the
world. Under our very eyes do we not see the
revolution spreading which modern machinery, and
particularly the steam engine, have effected? The
echoes of this invention are far from dying down.*

The Omnipotence of Dream

Distances are shortened. This Europe of ours, re-
duced in size by the extreme rapidity of communi-
sations, is really no larger now than France was
under the First Empire. At this moment the whole
world is not much larger than little Europe was a
century ago. What imminent changes in the his-
tory of the world this truth foretells!

Then there is the prodigious rise of books, pam-
phlets and newspapers, which scatter everywhere
the most daring ideas. Do they not hasten the com-
ing changes? It is not only by inventions that the
dreamers change the existence of their fellow-men,
but by ideas and speculations which seem most use-
less. Copernicus proves that the earth is not sta-
tionary. He drives it from that central position
which it so proudly occupied. It is nothing more
than a frail wanderer through infinity. Consider
the deep repercussions of this change. Since man
no longer dwells at the immovable centre of the
world, since he wanders over a little drop of mud
lost in the immensity of space, he is no longer lord
of the universe. He is losing his theological assur-
ance. Doubt, criticism, and all the fruitful rest-
lessness of modern times are getting under his skull.
A poor creature, most uncertain and very pitiable,
he realizes a little better every day the sancitity of
tolerance and mutual compassion.

[243]

The Opinions of Anatole France

Darwin teaches the law of evolution. Think of the unlimited influence it will henceforth exercise upon the mind. Constantly the mind feels more and more the profound, original sympathy which unites all that lives and suffers. Constantly it understands more clearly that everything is gradually changing, and that it is useless to try to stop the tide of inevitable change, or to hasten it. Thus most of the great discoveries end by acting upon our daily existence.

And the other dreamers, the writers and the artists—have they not as much power as the scientists? In truth, it is they who guide the people from above and in advance, since they form or clarify the mind of each nation. Without the intervention of the poets, how would the moral unity of a country be born? How would a common idea emerge from the diversity of races, the extraordinary differences of the provinces, brought together at haphazard by conquests and treaties, if the thinkers did not elaborate it together, and then for all their compatriots in turn? First of all, some dreamers express the feelings of the people about them: they become the mouthpiece of those who toil and rejoice beside them. Then, if their words are clear, if their natal domain imposes its law by wisdom or by force upon neighbouring territories, those first poetic accents

The Omnipotence of Dream

are transmitted like echoes to other bards, who take them up and spread them.

Gradually over the whole area of a country an agreement is reached, a harmony is composed, all dissonances are resolved in a single melody. Many dreamers, many poets, many artists take part in this concert. Yet from century to century, the leaders of the orchestra are few. There are not many Villons, Rabelais', Montaignes, Molières and Voltaires. . . .

To change the metaphor, these great men are the master-builders who construct a nation. At the call of their genius, hundreds and thousands of journeymen respond. In this way the character of a State is defined. Thus our spiritual motherland grew up, an edifice of independence and sincerity, of ironic wit and deadly mockery, an edifice of reason, of sociability, of pity, an edifice of human fraternity.

Now, my friends, we must continue bravely to build up this lovely edifice. This is not the time to stand by with folded arms. It must be enlarged that it may receive the whole world. That is the task of the dreamers, great and small. In order to see the walls rising, the proud colonnades and broad façades outlined, the humblest workman will joyfully climb the ladders, and carry the hod full of

The Opinions of Anatole France

*mortar to the more skilled labourers, who are lay-
ing the stones at the top of the scaffolding.*

*Therefore, my friends, let me mix the mortar,
let me mix the mortar, for the City of Dream.
That is my destiny; I like it, and I ask no other.*

THE END

Printed in the United States
72949LV00004B/11